CONSPIRING WITH FORMS 5/20/13

Gregg:
Best of luck
— and smooth
sailing —
in your own
conspiracy!

Terry

terry caesar

CONSPIRING with

FORMS

life in academic texts

the university of georgia press

athens & london

© 1992 by the University of Georgia Press | Athens, Georgia 30602 | All rights reserved | Designed by Richard Hendel | Set in Linotype Walbaum by Tseng Information Systems, Inc. | Printed and bound by Thomson-Shore, Inc. | The paper in this book meets the guidelines for permanence and durability of the Committee on Production Guidelines for Book Longevity of the Council on Library Resources. | Printed in the United States of America

96   95   94   93   92   C   5   4   3   2   1
96   95   94   93   92   P   5   4   3   2   1

Library of Congress Cataloging in Publication Data
Caesar, Terry.
   Conspiring with forms : life in academic texts / Terry Caesar.
   p. cm.
   Includes bibliographical references.
   ISBN 0–8203–1421–8 (alk. paper). — ISBN 0–8203–1494–3 (pbk.: alk. paper)
   1. Caesar, Terry. 2. English teachers—United States—Biography. 3. English philology—Study and teaching (Higher)—United States—History—20th century. I. Title.
PE64.C34A3 1992
820'.71'173—dc20
[B]   91-5028
                                                                                                         CIP
British Library Cataloging in Publication Data available

"Drifting Through the MLA" reprinted by permission from *Raritan: A Quarterly Review*, Vol. X, No. 2 (Fall 1990). Copyright 1990 by *Raritan*, 31 Mine St., New Brunswick, NJ, 08903.

"On Teaching at a Second-Rate University" originally appeared in the *South Atlantic Quarterly*, Vol. 90, No. 3 (Summer 1991). Copyright 1991 by Duke University Press.

CONTENTS

Preface | vii

Acknowledgments | xxix

1 Absence in Letters of Recommendation | 1

2 Whom to Acknowledge? | 28

3 Lack of Application | 50

4 Croaking About Comp | 69

5 Drifting Through the MLA | 87

6 Being a White Male | 103

7 On Not Writing a Dissertation | 125

8 On Teaching at a Second-Rate University | 145

Notes | 167

PREFACE

I DON'T KNOW when I became aware, writing these essays, that I was writing about myself. The one on dissertations I wrote years before the rest. Later I revised and enlarged it into something, no matter how personal, that I intended to be a meditation on dissertations generally. I had in mind not so much what was distinctive about my own experience as what was typical of it, or of what my own untypical process of writing a dissertation permitted me to see of the moment in every dissertation that is forced, arbitrary, and unwritten. Only gradually did I come to realize that this moment deployed for me the most fugitive space for institutional or disciplinary energies. The realization of this same moment seems to have propelled me to write each of the subsequent essays. By the last one, on second-rate universities, I wondered very consciously if the moment is finally the only thing I wanted to confront. But I never wanted to write about myself, even if, as we read in a recent Richard Howard poem, "an attempt to escape self / is likely to be identical with / an attempt to discover it."

I sent the one on letters of recommendation to a friend. He surprised me by taking it to be a contemptuous assault on both such letters and the system that requires them. I submitted the article to *PMLA*. In rejecting it, one reader was similarly engaged by its subjective energies, commenting on the "unfocused complaint" as well as on the essay's competing purposes as "a practical appraisal of gender bias," a personal narrative, an "analysis of the constitution of the subject," and a reading of a series of letters. The rejection didn't please me. The characterization did. James Bennett has a consideration on how little the technique of the analytical essay has changed despite how much recent theory has celebrated the "fissure" of boundaries between literature and literary criticism: "the argumentative, analytic order seems to cling firmly to nonfiction prose."[1] Certainly the *PMLA* reader's response testifies to how all in the analytic essay must be subordinate to some central purpose—whose own purpose, in turn, is to contain other techniques rather than release them.[2] I mean none of the following essays to challenge the boundaries of discursive prose, and yet I fail to see how a technique that permits some competition among purposes necessarily means that the force of any single one is blunted. Bennett quotes another critic who laments that the power of the traditional essay will "silence those who would naturally write about literature in nonanalytic modes" (Bennett, 110). I only plead myself for a more generous indulgence in the analytic mode. For the rest, having one's own voice is what each of these essays is about.

One other thought from this same *PMLA* reader: my essay "strongly suggests a recent bout of job applications." Why would he or she say this? It is not merely because the reader did not have the benefit of another of the essays included in this volume, which reveals that I've been applying for a job since the moment I took the only permanent one I've ever had. There is no small irony in the first reason I can think of. The particular conventions of the textual practices in which my professional life has been embedded resolutely avoid narrative; the *PMLA* reader's attempt to supply one anyway only demonstrates, I would say, the limitations of these very conventions.

Another reason and perhaps less of an irony: the particular narrative conjured up is a cliché, and, moreover, represents exactly the sort of conventional thinking about the profession with which my essay tries to contend. And yet, and yet. There is unaccounted for subjective life in the essay. I believe it was about John Berryman's Anne Bradstreet that someone once complained of feelings that persist in belonging to the poet rather than becoming the property of the poem.

Another friend read my essay on letters of application and declared that what I'm in fact doing there is asserting my superiority to conventional standards of job-hiring and presuming my equality with the reader-as-prospective-employer while triumphing over any writer's abject relation to any reader by my belittling of the commonplace application letter. Such a reading astonished me. What I thought I had done was to discuss yet another important professional text—or textual practice—by using my own example. While writing this essay, I did not take myself to be dramatizing my own life by somehow employing another text as pretext. But who is to say? Another sentence and I could begin to sound like a *PMLA* reader. Even intentionality is out of fashion as an interpretive guideline. (That is, officially. Unofficially, well, the textual practice of the reader's report—whose author enjoys perfect impunity—is another I wish I had been able to consider in these pages.) All my life I've read writers declining any number of intentions that critics have attributed to them. Usually I've felt the writers were only being self-protective and disingenuous.

So, I came to conclude, perhaps my friend's reading is more accurate than I care to allow. And suppose I want to ponder, for example, how the very distance I myself flaunt from the subject of composition is in a sense the same distance I censure on the part of authors who acknowledge others? The relationships among these essays are full of such rewritings. The same themes recur, similar ideas are relocated, and a few favorite quotations are employed from different perspectives. Although I never would have written any one of the essays had I not tried to bring the most concentrated analysis I could to the subject, I have to acknowledge that, nevertheless, the subjective presence in each of them claims equal attention to the analysis. From this point of view, each essay is comparable to a certain sort of fictionalizing, and all of them together resemble a group of short fictions.

I present myself in a series of professional, academic discussions, then, as well as the subjects of each of these discussions in me. The writing is that of the discursive essay, which consistently works at the edge of various formal conventions because I'm very insistent about wanting to represent experience *as* experience. Perhaps the most important reason letters of recommendation or second-rate universities are never discussed is that it's very difficult to do so without giving personal examples, telling anecdotes, naming names, and exposing contradictions. In "What English Departments Do," his seminal chapter of *English in America*, Richard Ohmann mentions in a footnote, for example, that he has chosen to omit "identifying clues" from the minutes that he quotes of a department meeting of a midwestern university in deference to "the violation of decorum" raised for two members of the department.[3] Something more clearly pointed than "decorum" was involved in the story Ed Cohen relates about how he had to drop the word "gay" from the title (among other changes he was asked to make) of his recent article on Oscar Wilde in order to get it accepted.[4] Reading Cohen, I recall the first chapter of *Homo Academicus*, where Pierre Bourdieu considers the problem of exemplification as one of the "special difficulties involved first in *breaking* with inside experience and then in reconstituting the knowledge which has been obtained by means of this break." The result of "subjective information" is that it invariably results in "reducing to the realm of ordinary knowledge those scientific constructs which had been painstakingly wrested from it."[5] What are the costs of this studious avoidance of the "ordinary?" One of them is that specificity suddenly looks exceptional and acquiescence becomes common sense.

So it's deemed just foolish to discuss certain things or to discuss them in certain ways. In a footnote Bourdieu mentions how early readers asked for examples regarding analyses "from which I had deliberately excluded all 'anecdotal' information"—the very information, he adds, "that journalists and popular essayists are most eager to reveal" (Bourdieu, 279).[6] I mention this example on examples because my own procedure is calculated to continue the very difficulties Bourdieu is anxious to assure his reader that he has eased by his very consciousness of them. I've assumed that it's important to name universities and to reveal something more of the narrative out of which an academic text emerges.

That is, I haven't wanted to "break" with inside experience. Of the subjects that I treat, only composition and dissertations are much written about, and then done so only as a consequence of removing the most personal cost of either the teaching or the doing. My own considerations of each of these subjects aim to restore the cost—and, I suppose, to demonstrate that without some account of the individual investment that one makes any "reconstituted" knowledge is too thin; it is "scientific" in the worst sense, that is, subject to statistics and altogether abstracted from the "ordinary" accidents that attend any human endeavor. One doesn't have to detest teaching composition as much as I do in order to acknowledge, I hope, that teaching composition is a radically incomplete project if those who detest it are effaced or repressed in the discourse about it. Similarly, one doesn't have to have my own strange history of writing a dissertation to realize that too many possibly even stranger stories are lost in the exquisitely rationalized and bureaucratized imperatives to do a dissertation in the first place. Undoubtedly many scandals have attended dissertations. Some occasionally appear in Bourdieu's popular press. Composition is a scandal, but not in the way it's normally publicized. The point I would make about so much of the experience having to do with each of these subjects, however, is that it has been formally "settled" as inside its special context only, and then eventually so far inside that what is vital, raw, or disaffected never gets out because it's not allowed to count for knowledge at all.

Therefore I've been very conscious, writing each of these essays, of wanting to *expose* something. But what precisely? Are there somehow constraints against considering acknowledgments in books? If so, are they the same ones in force against treating second-rate universities? What I've tried to do is not be too conscious of the theoretical solicitations provoked by these very questions. This is the reason, I believe, that my repeated references to Stanley Fish amount to an indeterminate conversation only. One could cite his distinction between "thinking with" and "thinking within" a practice: "To think within is to have one's very perception and sense of possible and appropriate action issue 'naturally' . . . from one's position as a deeply situated agent. . . . To think with a practice—by self-consciously wielding some extrapolated model of its working—is to be ever calculating just what one's obligations are, what procedures are 'really' legitimate, what evidence is in fact evidence, and so on."[7] But I don't find the difference as decisive as Fish does, in part because these days to think "within" is too inextricable from thinking "with." For instance, is part of being a "deeply situated agent" nowadays to read Fish? Or is one only shallowly situated if one doesn't? Come to this, how shallow does one have to be before one isn't really "situated" at all? I've met people who've never heard of Fish. Are these the same people who've never made any proposals to conferences? Are they incapable, nonetheless, of wondering if there wasn't a journal that would think to print a discussion, complete with real examples, of the teaching observations colleagues are now commonly asked to write up about each other? I suppose I can finally only speak for myself, for these questions occur to me, and here I must plead for a full Fishian wink, naturally.

Of course, from some more impersonal disciplinary perspective, it is easy to see that the profession of English has been resolute in ignoring any consideration of many of its most constituent textual forms. Why? I find Evan Watkins on the ins and outs of this question more insightful than Fish. One of the crucial distinctions in *Work Time* is the emphasis "on what circulates *in* English rather than what circulates from English."[8] Most of the texts I treat—letters of recommendation, dissertations, acknowledgments—are not exclusive to English and, perhaps more important, do not circulate as they do "from" English. So the profession disdains critical consideration of them because other texts (preeminently composition themes, among those included here) are far more crucial to its particular ethos of professionalism, as opposed to that which English shares with all other professions that impel their subjects to dissertate or to be recommended. Watkins is also very good on this ethos. After quoting Robert Scholes, he comments that we offer to students "the services of a professional liberationist. Thus social function [Scholes is urging an expanded textual study for greater individual understanding] suspended in the dissociation of value 'in itself' from value 'in circulation,' reemerges as utopian promise."[9] My simple point here can be put still more simply: discussion of letters of application or sessions at conferences appears to offer no liberationist potential.

The profession has been slow to recognize any other, even, surprisingly, during a time of immense theoretical license for the study of anything written. "My wager is that looking at the conditions under which people are hired, given tenure, published, awarded grants, and feted would repay the effort," writes Paul Rabinow. He continues with a list of questions: "How are careers made now? How are careers destroyed now?"[10] But Rabinow is writing as an anthropologist, and he compares such "issues" to fieldwork. Despite Linda Brodkey's chapter implicitly comparing the disciplinary subject to the ethnographic one, it may be that English suffers from the lack of empirical data about such questions because its own "ethos" is hostile to collecting it and instead far more receptive to grand, paradoxical theorizing such as Fish's. (I had a colleague who tried to conduct a nationwide survey of English departments concerning something or other. "I've got a lot of numbers," he eventually told me, "but I don't know how to interpret them." I don't think his heart was in it.) It cannot be merely that, for example, Ohmann's own "fieldwork" sample of departmental memos and minutes has discouraged others. And it seems to me too programmatically political to claim that determinable interests are being served because of the fact, for example, that the model to write grant proposals can be learned but the example of one submitted cannot be theorized. (Part of the reason is that apparently no one has thought to try to publish one—most provocatively, I would think, an unsuccessful one.)

Another example. A while ago I had to grade the midterm tests of two large intro to lit sections. Afterward I wrote a short essay about it. (It wound up being about how lost to the students is the private, isolated, fugitive, and irresponsible figure of the professor as opposed to "the person who strides into the classroom with all the tests completed as if nothing deeply questionable has happened at all.") I couldn't get it published. Was this because I had written on something else nobody writes about? (It's not very interesting to conclude that the essay just wasn't any good.) Or is it just that nobody writes about grading tests for good reason? Could we have reached a point where we already have enough examples of textualizing to study? Are tests just too concrete, too circumstantial, too ephemeral?

Careers are made on the basis of answers to such questions. Many of the chapters in this book consist of the study of academic forms that have abided so long as answers to questions that it's hard to recall the questions. Let me take another example, the matter of proposals, simply at the conference level. Conference calls for papers typically solicit something called "proposals," often defined as "abstracts" of one or two pages. But what is the form of a proposal? Consider Gayatri Spivak, who reprints "two documents" in a recent collection of essays on the new historicism: program notes for an MLA session and a telephone conversation with the editor. "Perhaps I am making a virtue of necessity," she writes, "but it seems to me entirely appropriate that it should be so."[11] One of the things I understand Spivak to be saying is that, since she is a Famous Critic, it is in her power to deem necessities to be at one with her occasions; so if she wants to print notes, she prints notes—for a session at which her appearance was of course the consequence of invitation, not competition. Hence the notes she prints don't actually constitute a proposal at all, neither in the procedure nor in the content by which most others in the profession are obliged to submit them for possible acceptance to heads of sessions at conferences. What can one so obliged conclude about this state of affairs?

He can turn to Fish for enlightenment, only to discover that the state of affairs is pretty much whatever the practice of Famous Critics deems it to be. (Geoffrey Harpham very acutely notes that "Fish has made his living from qualities more typically associated with careers in sports or venture capital: agility, pugnacity, tenacity, opportunism, inventiveness, risk, flair.")[12] "Ours is a hierarchical profession in which some are more responsible for its products than others," Fish cautions, "... there will always be those whose words are meritorious (that is, important, worth listening to, authoritative, illuminating) simply by virtue of the position they occupy in the institution." A bit later he is still more blunt about why a Spivak gets to publish her notes as notes: "There are words that matter more than other words spoken by those who address a field that they themselves have in large part constituted" (Fish, *Doing*, 166–68). For such worthies there is a real sense in which the form of a text doesn't really matter at all, for their practice sets the limits for, among other things, textuality itself. Barbara Hernstein Smith salutes Fish as "a disrupter and a maintainer of institutional structures—and, at all times, a master of border negotiations."[13] It falls upon the rest to have to work within his limits, and, alas, often get stopped at the border, if only because they lack the right papers. So many have to write "proper" proposals because a few don't. Many, for that matter, don't get to publish anything because a few others do.

How self-interested am I in pointing this out? As much as, say, Spivak? She might be more unsettled by the question than Fish, yet she scarcely has to acknowledge her self-interest as such at all, for her notion of "appropriateness" presumably has to do with the more grand question of her relation to her field than to herself. (Unless, that is, we adopt Fish's happy logic by which the two are revealed to be the same.) In *Discerning the Subject* Paul Smith states the following: "A person is not simply the *actor* who follows ideological scripts, but is also an *agent* who reads them in order to insert him/herself into them—or not."[14] Sometimes, writing these essays, it's seemed to me that I've wanted to read myself out of various "ideological scripts" more than to insert myself into them. This is an easier desire to sustain when one is already read out in fundamental ways from a field that partially consists of certain Greats, who, furthermore, inform one that the "script" that abides for the rest is not the product of ideological critique but of inevitable hierarchy. It could be argued that one powerful consequence of this "script" is that the proscribed way to comprehend it is to talk about the difference between "thinking with" and "thinking within" a practice. Certainly, in such a professional setting, only from above can self-interest afford to be confident, munificent, casual, and, of course, theoretical.

There is a lovely moment in Don DeLillo's *White Noise* when Jack Gladney's friend, Murray, salutes him for his seminal role in the establishment of Hitler Studies: "Nobody on the faculty of any college or university in this part of the country can so much as utter the word Hitler without a nod in your direction, literally or metaphorically."[15] Gladney's interest, in other words, *is* that of the field. What are the rest to do who cannot accomplish such a rare equivalence? Celebrate the transcendence of those who can, as a function of defining themselves, in turn, through them? One thinks of Thomas Mann's pronouncement to the effect that we all live under the name of the Great Invalid without whose madness we would ourselves be mad.[16] But the Great Critics appear before us, on the contrary, in perfect health, and they assure us that all is well by virtue of the fact that the profession has never been comprehended so well. It may be that it is given to the rest to have *only* various degrees of self interest, while the Great Critics exercise an agency so strong that no account of self-interest as such, or perhaps even of a self, need be presented.

I fear, very much on the contrary, that I will be accused of presenting only a self. That is, at least in part anyway, my various occasions are politically and socially thin for all their theoretical inflections. A reader for a composition journal wrote about my discussion of comp, for example, that "I've heard most of the croak before, albeit in more political language." I could reply in a number of ways—the most instinctive being that I deliberately intend the following essays to be a testing of exactly what sort of discourse about American higher education, most broadly, or English departments, most narrowly, is possible once what is left out of "political language" is *restored*. Another reason I can risk being politically thin is that Watkins is so heavy. *Work Time* is in many ways the nearest book I know to this one. I've learned much from it and at various places in my own text I've been tempted to use, say, the Gamscian notion of a discursive "war of position," which Watkins employs so acutely, or his repeated invocation of the idea of education as "compensation" for social inequality. Furthermore, I believe that several of my separate discussions could have positioned themselves more centrally around the function of English as what Watkins likes to refer to as the social circulation of people. Of course, on the other hand, one doesn't need to read Watkins to understand that universities didn't invent the ideology that makes it possible for some to dominate others or to feel that composition is an excellent example of a practice that provides certain kinds of "surplus value" (for example, how to fit into a group, these process days, as well as how to organize paragraphs) for the larger, postindustrial society.

I'm not sure, however, that some idea of "the marketplace" very helpfully explains why some get jobs (or books, conference papers, and Fulbrights) while others don't. I'm not sure what does. I'm only confident that if I give a careful, specific, and even personal account of some of these things, more will be disclosed than in any more overtly political context I could try to work up, especially since the more narrowly academic context that is my province is so good at interiorizing, conventionalizing, and textualizing the blunter political energies that it both takes from and gives to the larger society. From my own perspective it's fascinating to observe how Watkins seeks to submerge himself in institutional formation in order to study it, and yet fails; so he mentions his own semester teaching schedule, recalls a conversation with his mother, or tells a story about a friend from junior high who works in a bakery. One could find that the whole *direction* of *Work Time* is away from academic life entirely, because this life recuperates all resistance in the process of trivializing the "local yield" and has already occupied all the "positions" with fully rationalized logics of "conversion," no matter the "war." Certainly it's no accident, and Watkins knows it, that he concludes by talking about bakeries and popular culture. I think it's even less of an accident, although Watkins may not know it nearly as much, that even at the end he doesn't talk very explicitly about himself, a tenured Stanford professor who writes a formidably theorized and politicized book that uses *fuck* in it.[17]

As I write this I come across mention of a paper, from a recent conference, entitled "Gender-Based Alternatives to One-to-One Conferences." I mention it to a woman I know. "What it's about is simple," she opines. "The women professors get to fuck the female students now." I find her remark funnier than I probably should. I think I know why: I love forms, and I probably love violating them even more. Many academics do.

It's difficult to find the proper language. My own avoidance of overt or extended political reference is in part a choice not to use a certain idiom because it limits the fun of formal contemplation. Of course I want a vocabulary to get at more precisely the exquisitely abstract dispositions of higher education or the intricately mediated structures of the profession of English. But I don't just want to criticize these things. Although there's no illusory free place outside the realm of the political, nonetheless I want to play with forms, I want to get lost in them. I am, in a fundamental sense, lost in them.

An example. A couple of years ago I decided to try for an NEH Summer Stipend. You need two references. I assumed, mistakenly, that the grant is easy to get. So I saved my best references and instead asked two less exalted friends. One disappointed me by pleading lack of time; however, he offered to type up the recommendation if I'd write it myself and send it to him. I did, reluctantly. Maybe my reluctance explains why I added a postscript in which I wrote: "Just tell them, 'give him the fucking thing.'" Of course I was joking. In due course my friend sent me a copy of the recommendation he'd actually typed and signed. To my horror, he'd included my postscript. Only one slight change: like a good academic, he'd changed "fucking" to "frigging." I didn't get the grant.

The first thing that occurs to me in considering how to write about this incident is a question: how to theorize a grant application? Let me start with the following context from Watkins: "English is crucially positioned . . . in the distribution and certification of human capital resources, and whatever strategies of political praxis we can deploy occur precisely there" (Watkins, 271). A grant application, therefore, is both an exemplification of such positioning and an acquiescence to it. Furthermore, about these resources, Ohmann contends that, because of the existence of English in "hegemonic process," "we have helped inculcate the discipline—punctuality, good verbal manners, submission to authority, attention to problem-solving assignments set by someone else, long hours spent in one space—necessary to perform the alienated labor that will be the lot of most."[18] I can conclude that my above application represents a veritable comedy of alienation, then—but this is the problem: the comedy is lost to the alienation in a strictly political account. I don't want to lose it. Moreover, I would prefer to speak instead of "cheating," because I fear that too much is undisclosed in any political take about how often—I hope—some attempt is made by individuals to use their discipline in order to master their alienation, if not to undermine the hegemony which necessitates it.

I take the word *cheating* from Roland Barthes's last published interview, wherein he explained "the rebirth of individualism that would be more radical and enigmatic than the petit-bourgeois variety" by stating: "You can only do it by cheating, by clandestine behavior, undogmatic, non-philosophical behavior—by cheating, I can't find another word for it."[19] I can't find another word either, although I can think of plenty other examples, some my own, including one where I succeeded in getting a phony letter of recommendation I wrote into the file of a fictitious candidate for a departmental position. (Alas, he missed the final cut.) Or should I mention instead the time I explored with another very real candidate whom I hardly knew how she could sue the university because of an especially egregious series of hiring procedure violations by my department? This might seem more "political." I'm not sure it ultimately is. Staring at the white lines in a military prison DeLillo's Lee Harvey Oswald thinks: "The point of the brig was to clean the brig."[20] There is more than one way to clean the brig. You don't have to remember while doing so that the institution exists in order to imprison people. I will allow that few of my subsequent examples are nonphilosophical enough. I'm still learning how to cheat.

After such ignorance, what agency? My own particular agency in this volume is obviously not of some exceptionally authoritative kind. Therefore I've assumed that I need to give some account of myself, rather along the lines suggested in

Teletheory when we read of a critic's praise for a director's film: "It assumes the voice of personal consciousness at the same time it examines the very category of the personal" (Ulmer, 57). And yet I've come to acknowledge that the selfhood established in each essay in this volume is, as a general condition, the strongest claim to agency I can make. So be it. Truth lies, after all, in who says something, and under what circumstances, and not just in what is said. For me, the main curiosity of Smith's strenuous examination of dominant treatments of the subject in contemporary theory is that it establishes no self at all. (The main curiosity of Watkins's strenuous avoidance is that he fails to disestablish a self even if he has no "category" for it.) "So where is the subject?" Smith, at the end of the book, quotes a colleague as asking. He answers: "For the most part I've wanted to not answer this question; rather I've tended to displace it" (Paul Smith, 153). So have I. But not as much and not for the same reasons. Smith abstractly considers a distinction between actor and agent that I would have my own example confound, if not disallow. I must trust that the reader of these essays, at any rate, will know where the subject is.

A more interesting, if less marked, moment in Smith is registered on his last page. He has been "continually haunted" by the following "little passage" in Adorno's *Negative Dialectics*: "Suffering is objectivity that weighs upon the subject; its most subjective experience, its expression, is to be objectively conveyed" (Paul Smith, 160). I could develop my difference from Smith in the following way. I provide a more explicit account of my own displacement because I work through a series of textual or discursive instances that each situates how I am to be myself displaced as a subject. The essence of this displacement, furthermore, is that it be, each time, conducted according to objectified criteria. Smith's quoting Adorno is most acutely read as a cry that too much of his own most subjective experience, on the other hand, has had to be lost to his discourse about theoretical, that is, "objective," conveyance.

I want to be clearly understood: suffering is not an issue in

Preface | xxi

any of the following essays. Instead it is simply the result of being a subject at all. This said, however, I think it has to be added that academic life so consummately constructs, or constricts, itself according to Adorno's definition of suffering that any account of academic life will perforce be an account of suffering. This doesn't mean it's any worse than others and even very bad in comparison to most; I concur with Watkins (whose own last page is about suffering) when he states that "work in English for a permanent labor force does not mark a comprehensive system of humiliation as work does for so many others" (Watkins, 276). Nevertheless, suffering is what discarded or disused subjectivity is all about. I would have any reader of my chapter, "On Not Writing a Dissertation," compare it with a recent article, "The Ph.D. Squid" by Theodore Ziolkowski.[21] The author's discourse is so magisterially above his own experience (unmentioned) of having written a dissertation that one feels mean-spirited to wonder anyway how he himself managed it, much less how his discourse might be affected if he did not presume a dissertation as something to be "managed." I don't mean to imply that Ziolkowski is any less authoritative because subjective nuance is so effaced from his objectivity. I do mean to imply that there is deep, curious, highly distinctive suffering at least likely in the writing of any dissertation as there is in so many aspects of academic life. You won't write very well about this life if you try to avoid its long, slow rhythms, its intricately tolerated bureaucratization, and its official pretense that "subjective experience" is embarrassing, compromising, and beside the point.[22]

There's even the pained consequence of being objectively weighted and freighted in the academy today if one is a man. Such a theoretically lamentable position is the subject of one of my essays. Here I only want to remark on how different my own "subject-position" would be if I were a woman. Not only would I be conceded a sort of routine victimization; my subjectivity would be distinguished by its very manifestation—hard-won, as is every other woman's, from the "phallocentric representationalism" (or some more felicitously named oppression) that never before permitted it to be expressed in its own name, mine. A few years ago, responding to another woman's essay about epistemological blindness in literary discourse, Jane Tompkins gave an unusually frank demonstration of how the whole notion of subjectivity can be taken over by feminist discourse, until, I would add, it becomes empowered only as a function of feminist discourse.

"The problem is that you can't talk about your private life in the course of doing your professional work," states Tompkins.[23] Hence, she sees herself as split between "critic" and "person," a split that is derived from a "public-private dichotomy," which is in fact a hierarchy. What to do with this "other" voice? Tompkins quotes Ursula LeGuin on the difference between the father tongue and the mother tongue, recalls the feminist tenet that the personal is political, agonizes about how she wants to break away from "my conformity to the conventions of male professional practice," records how she hates the way men treat women, and finally concludes that "it feels so good" to have written out how she both has had and will have to "deal with the thrashing of emotion, and with my anger against it" (Tompkins, 176, 178).[24] By the end, that is to say, her enunciative authority is entirely appropriated from feminism. Feminism, in addition, testifies to Tompkins's suffering (a word she doesn't use) and mediates its complaint.

My own subjectivity, very much in contrast, has at best a far more elusive "ideological script." (Of course insofar as it is understood as male, it is suspect.) It is much easier to conclude that it is merely mine alone. It has no other name than mine. Having no other name, it is inevitably "personal." I would go further and claim that feminism is the name it ought to have. (My chapter on this argues that feminism is the only name an avowedly male criticism can have.) Smith's last chapter, quite tellingly, awards to feminist theory the strongest, most sophisticated maintenance of the subject's dual claims both to some essence and to irreducible duplicities. It's all very well to offer the feminist subject as in this way exemplary. But in fact it's nearly impossible to imagine a man publishing, for example, Jane Gallop's *Thinking with the Body*, even in terms of its very title, much less its cover of a woman giving birth or such of its disclosures as masturbating while reading De Sade. Gallop's text enacts a most theoretically wily, knowing subjectivity in very careful moments because it can depend upon another "body" of feminist discourse that has already marked spaces for these moves and therefore made possible the exercise of an agency that can confidently give a mere gesture. One condition Smith gives for the political potential of "heterogeneity" is that "this recognition can only take place if the 'subject's' ability to refer to real conditions is unblocked by theory" (Paul Smith, 159). At the present time feminist theory, which in so many ways has been responsible for an immense release of all that it can most personally mean for a person to be a subject, nonetheless comprises the primary source of blockage for other representations of subjectivity, especially if they are those of a man.

Worse—setting aside here the special vexations of homosexuality—of a man who would insinuate himself into perhaps the most aggrieved subject-position of a woman: not having one's own voice. I think it a fact that many people besides women don't have their own voices, and you don't have to be a woman not to. Nor of course do you have to be embedded in an academic situation. (But it helps to have read Foucault: "The individual is not a *vis-à-vis* of power; it is . . . one of its effects.")[25] What you do have to be in order not to have a voice in an academic context is to be embedded *in a certain way*. Each of these essays attempts to define this way. None does so completely. None does so in terms of all the rest. Let me cite Smith once more, when he cautions that the "subject" no longer need be understood as equivalent to the "individual," and then speaks of "overlapping subject-positions" as "a more exacting, variable conceptualization of a person's history" (Paul Smith, 32). I have to assume that much of the provocation of reading all these essays lies in considering the overlap and being engaged by such questions as whether teaching composition and attending conferences, as I describe each, propose very different kinds of subject-positions after all. Indeed, my most active provocation might be whether there are too many such positions here, or too few, and how, in either case, both composition and conferences can be held accountable.

For me, the particular selection of professional moments assembled here reveals how vigilant an actor has to be on a certain kind of academic stage with a certain kind of script in order to arrogate to himself a more active, commanding kind of agency. (Do the analogies to sports I come up with in more than one essay clearly indicate one direction more than the other?) My fascination with the script is something about which I can't cheat. My ambition to publish more than a few lines of my allotted role is just as apparent. Prefaces to books never speak of how much the author wanted the book—how long it took to get it into print, over what obstacles, and at what cost; this preface to this one won't have to speak of any of this—most of the essays can be read in one sense as a species of apology either for not having been able to publish a book or perhaps for never having had a career that would have enabled a book to issue from it.

Compare, on this question, Richard Ohmann in his preface to *Politics of Letters*: "I wrote the essays in this volume over an eleven-year period, for various occasions and out of various exigencies. They come closer to carrying a single argument than I would have remembered had not Jeannette Hopkins of Wesleyan University Press suggested collecting them, and initiated this agreeable labor of words" (Ohmann, xiii–xiv). Few are more knowledgeable about the complexities of precisely what his title suggests than the author of *English in America*. Yet one wonders if he would have so blithely written the above words had he been fully mindful of how many in his potential audience could only read in wonder over his gesture at what for them is the failed dream of a lifetime. Ohmann discloses the best way to have it realized: to discover one's own book as already in the possession of someone else, who has only to reveal herself.

There is no knowing how many in the profession consider their careers failures because they succeeded in publishing no book. (Compare Sartre: "The history of a life, whatever it may be, is the history of failure.") Perhaps not as many do as I imagine. I'm not sure, for example, that my oldest friend from graduate school does. He's been outside the profession for a long time. Yet I believe that by now he'd take it to be a veritable affirmation of having lived if he got either of his two novels into print. I know another man, albeit less well, who really considers his one book such an affirmation. Are such things never mentioned in print (excluding biography) because they're too candid? Because they're unrepresentable? Or because they raise the specter of failure? One could muse that all the textualizing strategies assembled here can be taken as so many ways to keep away this specter: there's either a letter of recommendation or a conference for everyone, and if you can't get published you can at least get photocopied. Perhaps the singular instance of a book is no longer to many in the profession as it once was before dissertations were somewhat less significant and both government grants and classroom observation reports still less than that. Of course, as always, much depends on where you teach and if teaching is all you're expected to do.

A while ago at a conference I met a man with whom I had been a member in a summer seminar thirteen years before. We got to know each other pretty well then. I believe he may have been the first person I met who persuaded me that he taught at a worse place. Not only was his university woefully smaller and located in one of the most remote areas in the country; the previous semester he'd taught one of seven classes in another state. He swore then that he'd quit the profession if he didn't get out of where he was in two more years. "I didn't get out" was almost the first thing he said to me after we shook hands again. "Now I've got two kids and a house," he continued. "I may as well admit I'll be there forever." We didn't get to talk much more. I don't know if he's been able to publish. He doesn't have a book. Would he want to admit that his career has been a failure? What *lack*—of achievement, of mobility, of something—does the profession recognize as constituting failure?

Or, again, are there now so many measures of success that no one can be decisive if it's lacking (beyond tenure, which, significantly, is a procedure not susceptible to textual form)? In the terms that I treat in my last essay, the university that will forever contain the energies of my former colleague is abysmally second-rate. One way to define the term is to say that at second-rate universities failure arises from lack of stability, whereas at first-rate universities failure is the result of lack of recognition. My former colleague at least has stability. For him it may suffice. For me it never has. Hence the following essays consort with failure as perhaps no other subject—the application unanswered, the subject untaught, the institution unknown. But I don't directly discuss failure, which insinuates itself into so many unacknowledged texts here without ever coalescing into some clear, definite form of its own.

If I'd wanted to write straightforwardly about failure, I would have done so. I think I know why I haven't. Charles Altieri has an unusually searching review of *Discerning the Subject* in which he faults Paul Smith for a narrow sense of contestatory possibility: "For he never tells us why the tensions within agency should produce resistance rather than, say, eliciting more intense versions of a Barthesian jouissance that is delighted by precisely those contradictions and has no interest in resolving them."[26] This would, I think, be an excellent comment on Watkins as well; it's hard to recreate resistance as fun, and probably harder to theorize pleasure as a form of resistance. As for my own text, some have found humor, even comedy, in each of these essays. To me there's too much tension. I miss delight in all of them.

Failure? It only slackens the tension. At the end of his review Altieri finds Smith's discursive allegiances ultimately irresponsible. He makes, to my mind, a still more memorable criticism: "So if we are to idealize resistance, perhaps we might look closer to home, to the lies that our disciplinary practices allow us to maintain to ourselves" (Altieri, 263). One of these lies, presumably, is that our spaces for resistance are theoretical only and they serve to keep us away from others with whom we could discover either truer allegiances or more commonplace consolations. I want to think that I've written the following essays in the spirit of Altieri's demystifying injunction, and so there is not an essay on failure included here because it would be about too simple a truth and too devious a lie.

ACKNOWLEDGMENTS

ANYONE WHO has written a book that includes a chapter on acknowledgments in books faces a somewhat unusual problem in writing his own. In my case, the problem is compounded by the fact that I really have very little to mention—which is of course one reason why I wrote the chapter.

That is, in writing this book I had no support from any agency or foundation. I had no grants, no fellowships.

In addition, I had no released time or research help or funding of any kind from my university. Finally, the subjects of most of my chapters rather necessarily exclude students and more deviously exclude colleagues.

Already I've produced too unwittingly bleak a fiction. Let the bright side of my intention to write be represented in name by one person only, my wife, friend, colleague, and coconspirator, Eva Bueno, without whom I would not have become so acutely aware of all that is written, in more than one language, in order that nothing need be acknowledged.

CONSPIRING WITH FORMS

chapter one

ABSENCE IN LETTERS

OF RECOMMENDATION

POSSIBLY NO FORM of writing both consolidates and constitutes the profession of English more than letters of recommendation. These days, when even *PMLA* prints a consideration of cookbooks, much of the theoretical ground is cleared for a discussion by simply designating a heretofore unexamined writing practice as one which produces a *text*. Therefore, I want to stress at the outset that, although the formal properties of the text of recommendation are central to the following discussion, the institutional conditions in which this text is produced will be equally my concern. What I want to study is less the profession, however, than its confidential, but far from confident, textualization of itself as revealed in letters of recommendation. The most important thing such a study reveals may be that these letters are so apparently indispensable because their rhetoric, conventions, and even metaphysical assumptions continue to be both unspoken and untheorized. Letters of recommendation, in other words, may ultimately make very little sense as texts—and yet this is precisely why we continue to need them.[1]

A preliminary consideration: all in the profession write letters of recommendation, and all have them written about themselves, and yet few ever see any one of these letters because not one of them has any wider, public status beyond its individual occasion—a job, a grant proposal. Letters of recommendation are written to be filed not circulated. One reason I write is that I happen to have been in various positions during a single year that required me to review a great number of applications for both jobs and grants on local, state, and federal levels. I'll quote from them. I may have readers who'll recognize their own words. I must trust no one else will—and that anyone will understand that to name names or provide other specifics would only violate the conditions under which any of the letters was written and read. What I want to do instead is to analyze these conditions. None may be more decisive than that letters of recommendation are assumed to be privately written and privately read. I assume this does not mean they cannot be publicly discussed.

And an initial disclaimer: it is not my purpose here to write a disciplinary history in which the original space for the text of recommendation is located and explained. I don't know when the profession of English first came to require professors to profess other professors. In *The Rise and Fall of the Man of Letters*, John Gross mentions that when Edmund Gosse applied for the post of Clark Lecturer at Cambridge in 1880 he submitted "testimonials" from Tennyson, Browning, and Arnold. How common was this practice?[2] When did it become bureaucratized? Did it so become in precisely the same way in the United States as in England? These are important questions. It is more to my purpose here, however, to ask—I think rhetorically—whether letters of recommendation could be extracted from any institutional archive over any one year past, much less decades earlier? The Educational Rights and Privacy Act of 1974 certainly altered the confidentiality of such letters—but only on behalf of those about whom any one letter was written; nothing has altered in some larger sense, and anyone who might want to engage in a study of how post-1974 letters may have changed, for example, still has no wider access to any data. My point is that the history inscribed in letters of recommendation themselves, as they have accumulated in one academic discipline only, throughout the decades of this century alone, has never been available and will never be known.

I have spoken of conventions. Most basically, from what model is the text of recommendation derived? It is my sense that anyone who writes a letter of recommendation follows pretty much the same schema. Howard Gardner gives his (and gives it *as* his) in the following way: a first paragraph on the nature of his relationship to the individual to be recommended, a second on the nature of that individual's professional life, a third on scholarly accomplishments (Gardner mentions "an optional paragraph" on teaching abilities), a fourth on "personal dimensions," and a final, "summative" paragraph on both present and future assessments.[3] Rather than inquire into the institutional or disciplinary structures within which such a model has been deemed to be intelligible, I want to emphasize what the conventions are designed *not* to disclose: the recommended subject as a personal—contingent, circumstantial, bodily, or sexual—being. I've never read a letter of recommendation that quotes its subject. I can scarcely imagine one that would provide a physical description.

A while ago I read a letter of recommendation about a man who underwent chemotherapy while completing his dissertation. One or two on the committee of which I was a member were virtually scandalized, as each remarked individually to me. When we all met as a group, we never mentioned this letter. I was not a member of any group that convened when

I read another letter that stated that, earlier in the scholar's career, she had experienced "severe gynecological problems (now completely resolved)." This is another instance where the body is mentioned, the better to emphasize how character triumphed over it. Later I want to consider the special interpretive problems such inscriptions of the physical present in letters of recommendation. Here I want to emphasize how its effacement functions to represent the recommended candidate as a totalized being fully in possession of his or her resources, which are steadfastly inward and resolutely disciplined. Bourgeois virtues of health and temperance are always assumed. For all the rest, there may be marriages but no "marital troubles." Desire exists to be mastered.

Or rather desire exists to be elided into a disposition of the recommended subject, who is segmented into three parts: characterological, social, and intellectual. The boundaries that separate each of these from the others are not hard and fast; indeed, the ideal person who would emerge from the text of recommendation is a seamless unity of individual being, colleague, and scholar. It is the burden of the format that sets out this unity to ease the transition from one part to another by encouraging a certain amplitude of idiom that reveals how in fact each part is active in the others. Consider the following statement: "Dr. X is a talented faculty member in the Department of English who has made major contributions to our Department and to the College community during his five years here." Such statements are laudatory staples and can function in any paragraph; the "talent" assumes a kind of transcendental placement in the subject's being and the contributions can be assumed to be the more actual because they cut across any single manifestation of them. Again, ideally—for too great a manifestation in any one part argues for narrowness just as surely as some conflict between parts puts the case for condemnation—the recommended subject is all things to all peers and the same things to students as well. One is "never flashy or arrogant." Said of a personality, it could as well be said of a teaching style. Another "creates a wonderful learning environment." Located in the classroom, such a performance could easily be relocated in the department lounge. A third has "remarkable generosity." This desideratum is at once available as a quality of mind, of behavior, and of character. Few things are more crucial to the text of recommendation than to insure that its subject is all of a piece.

Consequently, few things are more interesting about this text than that its rhetoric reveals a carefully graded system of discriminations. The segmentation can in fact be assembled as a hierarchy, which the conventions that govern letters of recommendation allow to operate under the condition that the hierarchy be diffuse, incomplete, and continually renegotiable. How important is it that we have colleagues with whom we can get along? What sort of qualities do we want in a colleague? Are they the same sort as we want in fellow teachers we respect and admire? Whether inside or outside the classroom, is it more important to be "tireless" or to be "dynamic"? In what precise setting does something called "speculative intensity" work best, or are there occasions in which such a thing is not desirable at all? These questions are difficult—difficult to answer, difficult even to pose, and perhaps most difficult of all to admit, which is why letters of recommendation only do, as it were, by default, and then only in terms of the procedural agenda of a schema that itself admits of no clear derivation. There are departments where an individual is expected to be less that than a member of a group. There are others where a he is really supposed to be a she (or vice versa). There are fellowships or grants where teaching matters hardly at all and others where the institution in which the research has been done matters more than the research itself. Letters of recommendation have to address too many questions, too many occasions. It is crucial that they have the character of a technique rather than a form.

Techniques, after all, appear more malleable, enabling, utilitarian—tools for judgment, rather than constituents of judgment. Nonetheless, even the most unassuming technique has its proper rhetoric, and, in turn, this rhetoric's more strictly formal operation in letters of recommendation is motivated by the fact that any one letter is designed to permit a *verdict*. The text of recommendation may be empowered by an illusory unity for its (ideal) subject because everywhere outside the text there is effective disunity—often no agreement, not even about any of the questions, within individual departments as well as no possible agreement among departments because the separate needs among them don't add up. Furthermore, it may also be that the text of recommendation appears to disavow any hierarchization among its seemingly interchangeable parts because the peculiar nature of the verdict at which it aims is one that has to be remorselessly hedged, qualified, and deferred within bureaucratic structures. As Kafka writes in *The Trial*: "The verdict doesn't come all at once, the proceedings gradually merge into the verdict."

What I want to claim is that the recommended subject, already segmented into three parts, is, more importantly, a discursive subject whose social being is more significant than his or her character and whose intellectual being is more significant than his or her social being. The arrangement of these parts doesn't especially matter. The rhetoric does. Each of these three categories, no matter how fluid their presentation, has a distinctive rhetoric. In addition, the rhetoric of each of these categories appropriates what cannot be said in each of the preceding categories. Let me discuss each in sequence.

Of an ideal characterological profile, I think it is most important to assure that a requisite modesty is present. An individual is "modest but self-assured," to cite a formulation as close in any from letters of recommendation to being a formula. Other epithets such as "reasonable," "reliable," or even "thorough" and "lucid" are variations of praise for a primal modesty at which none are offended and in which all feel flattered. It is modesty that enables such commendations as the following: "He is a warm, personable, and caring individual. His relationships with students, administrators, and faculty are excellent." One could even speculate that it is modesty that guarantees how assertiveness remains admirable rather than abrasive, as in the following example: "She has assumed a leadership posture that has been fundamental to the institution's growth and pluralistic depth." Modesty is critical to having a "genial disposition." Modesty is so important that it can be attached, like a garland, to other things that could be normally taken in contrast to it, as in "modestly brilliant." Modesty is what takes the edge off being "stimulating."

Is modesty, in addition, a sanction for more exciting human possibilities? This is hard to say—as hard as these very possibilities are to assess or weigh. Certainly it is indisputable praise to write of someone as "a very lively presence," or of another who is "vigorous," or of still another who "energizes." But what about a subject of whom it can be written: "He teaches with a vengeance and an intensity?" Such a subject is, I think, potentially too powerful, too unsettling, and so such vivid nuances are rare in letters of recommendation. When a rhetoric of excitement is employed—or emotion, provocation, effect—a text of recommendation has shaded, overtly or not, into the representation of its subject as a social being. Or rather, the same social being its subject was on a characterological level is now transposed into bolder relief, as someone both more aggressively and more necessarily "interactive." Not only is this level a progression from the preceding because it provides a fuller manifestation of it; the rhetoric here is less formulaic, more searching. Put another way, a recommended subject actively situated in the social realm takes risks, and the discourse about such a subject is a measure of the risks that are taken, or, again, that need to be taken, if relations among men and women are to have interest, development, and energy.

Is the rhetoric employed to commend teaching a displacement of that which cannot be employed, nevertheless, about a social being? It is a fact, I believe, that the sheer *power* that one person may effect on others is represented in letters of recommendation finally only in terms of teaching. Outside the classroom, it suffices to praise someone as "enthusiastic." Enthusiasm, indeed, is modesty with far more vitality and no more menace. Inside the classroom, it is necessary to add that the enthusiasm is, say, "demanding"—that is, exactly the sort of thing it is outside the classroom but there more confusing, disturbing, and threatening. A teacher can be many things that a colleague cannot, with the proviso that the one role be subsumed in the larger, more varied, and more encompassing professional world where one says hello at the departmental coffee pot and makes telling comments at meetings.

Consider a letter in which Professor X is lauded as "one of the truly spectacular teachers" at his university, where his lecture courses are "unequalled in the loyalty they evoke from students." A student publication cites one for its "ability to raise challenging, inescapably moral questions." The text continues that its subject "combines extremely high standards for his students and a willingness to give them extraordinary attention [serious debate over spaghetti dinners is the materialist way to put it]. He is unstinting in his time and energy." Most of the rhetoric employed to commend classroom performance is registered here, and I must trust it will be noticed how different it is from that which represents behavior outside the classroom; outside, one could add, spaghetti dinners are of course actually eaten, during which time few prefer principles over pasta, and especially among colleagues, where one does not expect to be treated like a student. Inside, one is expected to be dynamic. This is so, if one were to understand solely in terms of the text of recommendation, because outside one is not expected to be dynamic.

It may of course be possible that the self-contained space of the classroom makes possible a display both of human potential and interaction too intense, concentrated, and focused to be sustained. It is nonetheless accurate, I believe, to say that the energies available for the rhetoric about teaching performance have been appropriated from their diminution, or attenuation, in the broader professional setting. Another text speaks of this last setting in the following very typical way: "He is extremely cooperative and is always willing to spend time helping students, developing new courses and participating on committees." Exactly. In the text of recommendation, *excess* abides in a continuum, or else there is something dubious and unbalanced about it. Along this continuum, no subject, no matter how apparently charismatic, preens, nor do her or his standards, no matter how exacting, ever grate. It is as if what is "spectacular" must be ceaselessly prepared to contract into something that is merely "extremely" what it is; this adverb, in the last-cited sentence, is another version of enthusiasm, which, as ever, mediates between the incitements (emotional and otherwise) of wayward, special realms and the imperatives of more mundane, social ones.

Yet what about incitements careless of any realm or restless finally only to be the creation of their own? "I must create my own system or be enslaved by another man's," pronounced Blake, and the fame of such a statement within the profession of English reveals all by itself a celebration of selfhood (including a host of attendant virtues, such as creativity or energy) that does not abide very happily within Kafka's "proceedings." Yet since these proceedings allow the discipline to be recreated in bureaucratic terms, how does a profession deal with its (albeit scholarly) Blakes?[4] They might get hired under the guise of being modest, but they don't get published this way. How then, much less how do they attain real professional distinction? In the text of recommendation, the only space for some sort of answer to such questions is the intellectual one. Somewhere I chanced to read the architect, Philip Johnson, explaining the success of a friend and colleague: "Chutzpah. He's a shit." What is chutzpah? What is its place in the scheme of socialization that the text of recommendation, as I have been discussing it, is mandated to set out? Can a bad man produce a good book? Or an even worse woman a better one? There is no question that letters of recommendation for the profession of English award their highest accolades for scholarly activity. What I want to emphasize is that, as a result of this fact, a whole rhetoric can function that recoups not only individualistic and careerist motivations that cannot be spoken about on preceding levels but also which concedes the presence of mean-spiritedness and defiance by effacing these things in the higher, official goals of intellectual achievement.

Rhetoric at this level is unusually subtle. Anyone who has read enough letters of recommendation notices that the very adjectives used to describe intellectual activity are different from any other kind—words such as "deft," "nervy," "tantalizing," or "provocative" contrast markedly with "personable," "cheerful," or "congenial." A project will be characterized as, for example, "intellectually spacious," not a behavior. One is commended for having one's ideas "deftly positioned," not one's colleagues. This much is rather obvious. Suppose, however, we consider such a statement as the following: "It is not often that one sees distinguished scholars taking off in radically new directions." The statement does not say why. The implicit question never appears as such. Nor do any social consequences of such radical enterprise. Indeed, "radical" is an honorific in this context, as it always is. In the text of recommendation, it is given to the life of the mind of the ideal subject never to be satisfied—and yet equally to be governed by a sure sense of purpose, in the above case the more profound because, distinction already reached, the less predictably complacent. Such "radicalism" does not have to be made explicit. In the following example it appears to be denied: "In a quiet, unobtrusive way, X has been laying the foundations for a major revision"—in our concept of something, of our understanding of something else, it hardly matters, rhetorically. One can rightly claim, I think, that this denial of radical manner is only an understated way of disclosing the true, deeper radical force.

It is at the shrine of this force, clothed in modesty and uttered with enthusiasm, that the text of recommendation seeks to worship. A major revision, a radical new direction: before such wonders the most effective teaching appears circumscribed and ephemeral, the most attractive character becomes tame and uninteresting. One reads of another recommended subject lauded for his "ability to make a particular text a paradigm for larger problems, and to situate his readings in relation to a wide variety of contending critical forces." The world inscribed in such letters is a world of force. Such worthy goals as cooperation attempt to routinize it, and such unexceptionable values as commitment strive to idealize it. Ultimately, though, force occupies—or at least is implicated in—all positions and positionings by the unquestioned authority of its high brutality, and the man or woman who incarnates this force is accorded the authority, in turn, of something equivalent to a disciplinary formation.[5]

To describe this last point more thoroughly, I want to analyze one of the most interesting letters of recommendation I've ever read. It begins with an unusually acute paragraph that stages its own warrant, and, in the process, reviews the hierarchical configuration whose progression I've been tracing:

> Academic departments are a conglomeration of three kinds of people: the hangers-on who do their jobs well enough year after year; the active participants who will help out with any project, volunteer often and contribute unlimited time and energy to 'worthy' department enterprises; and those who by instinct or conscious thought manage from within to reshape and provide new direction for the department by their own activities and projects, adding fresh dimensions and challenging hints of what might be.

There is a final, predictable sentence: the recommended subject belongs to the latter group.

Notice, first of all, how this latter group, although aligned with the other two, represents a much less collective project for which motivations are not clear and purposes are almost indeterminable. Therefore, the kind of determination the text gives this project has, I think, the status of a necessary fiction. Clearly there are energies in this latter group that must be deployed as socially useful, even if they are not social in substance. (It is this sort of tension that makes letters of recommendation for jobs much more fully compelling, and this is why I have been concentrating almost exclusively upon these, rather than letters for grants or fellowships.) A department is a department because it can appropriate such energies, although it is also a department because, in a far more obscure and maybe insidious sense, it has such energies "in" it.

The text continues in a conventional manner: its subject is "soft-spoken, thoughtful, self-assured," he agreeably took on an additional assignment, and so on. Then comes the penultimate paragraph:

> Issues are important to X. But equally important is the way issues are solved. He is a research-oriented teacher who understands the value of empirical evidence, careful methodology and the decision-making process. He is deeply interested and professionally committed. . . . His decision to develop [here follows a brief characterization of major research] is not the result of a whim or a capricious decision to "find a project." It comes from his intense concern as a humanist/scholar/teacher who cares about the people and the world around him, who tries to interpret issues for himself as well as for others.

There are many features worth considering here: the yoking together of activities and roles elsewhere kept apart, the hedging about of convictions and values as if they must not appear to conflict, and the converging, first of man into work, then of work into ethic lest there appear to be some confusing pressure among them. This is, again, a text almost too consciously in command of its rhetorical options, and here almost too dense for seeming to want to choose them all.

What I find most significant is that this paragraph even marks what most texts of recommendation normally suppress: the possibility that none of the rest of what it says matters, for its subject's dedication could be a tissue of whim and caprice. Of course it's not; that's the point of the letter. Nonetheless, surrounded with professional urgencies, lodged amid disciplinary programmatics, and then denied, the specter of utter self-interest is not completely banished once it is theoretically proposed. Indeed, to see it so rarely mentioned is enough to set loose the speculation that the whole text of recommendation might operate for the sole, final purpose of dispelling the scandal of a subject who is immodest, uninterested, and unrecuperable even by the highest criteria of the profession, which are, perhaps more horribly, intimate with the very lowest standards.[6]

"Professional socialization aims, in fact," writes M. S. Larson, "at the internalization of special social controls; it takes, that is, standards defined by the profession's elites and makes them part of each individual's subjectivity. Insofar as this socialization is successful, the elites will be in control not only of material rewards but also of the kind of esteem that counts—the esteem granted by a reference group of major importance to the individual."[7] Yet what if the socialization isn't successful? What if an individual only cares about material rewards, or elite esteem in order to get material rewards? For the text of recommendation, such questions are bad enough at any level, but worst at the scholarly pinnacle, where a subjective center is celebrated and yet where, exactly because of this, there may be subjective elements completely elusive of (if not parasitic on) social controls. What if a project were mere whim or caprice? The text of recommendation—whose very existence is arguably part of "elite control"—can only reply in the negative; that is, if it is to function in any recommendory mode at all.

A final possibility: what if whether or not a project is a product of whim or caprice simply *doesn't matter*? If so, then what does? Very simply: the Great Work. (Compare Cyril Connolly, who once stated that the true function of a writer is simply to produce a masterpiece.)[8] The major revision, the radical new direction: again, the profession depends on these—just as departments depend on those who reshape it from within—and theoretically any project might result in such reconfigurations, which are so vital that the project, in turn, has the force of an end in itself. What matter if vanity or opportunism provides the motive force for such an end? There are moments in letters of recommendation when such potentialities are disclosed, especially when they become so real they have to be summoned into the text in order to be banished. I wish I could cite a better example than that immediately above. Of course no text of recommendation can be conceptually adequate to such moments. What has to be stressed instead is the character of intellectual—not to say disciplinary—life as an integrative rather than divisive thing; scholarly work must be all of a piece with the rest, despite the presence within it of uniquely disruptive, exploitive, and egotistic opportunities, all of which appear in the text of recommendation in another register.

The professional role of this text is only to monitor (and therefore regulate) activity. However, in the process an exemplary type is produced, whose individual excesses or professional eccentricities provide such a discretionary challenge for a writer to mention that a reader of the text necessarily enters into a very real complicity with it in order to read it at all. Why is this so? Whose authority ultimately governs the text? How is a letter of recommendation different because it is about an actual person? I want to take another section in order to consider these questions.

2

Perhaps the most famous example of a letter of recommendation in a fictional text is in *Invisible Man*. The letters that Dr. Bledsoe gives the narrator to assist his temporary dismissal (he thinks) from college after the fiasco with Mr. Norton are not precisely those I've been considering, and of course they function in no similar disciplinary circumstances, but nonetheless I believe they will serve to dramatize one thing about any general text of recommendation. Recall that the son of the last trustee whom the narrator tries to see gives him a copy of the letter to read. It declares that the bearer has been expelled, bids its addressee to continue the narrator in the delusion that he has not been, and further requests that he be more generally assisted in the illusion that he can make something of his life. Subsequently the narrator recasts the letter as follows: " 'My dear Mr. Emerson,' I said aloud. 'The Robin bearing this letter is a former student. Please hope him to death, and keep him running. Your most humble and obedient servant, A. H. Bledsoe.' "[9]

In other words, letters of recommendation can be vicious and lie. Yet readers are normally in no position to verify what one says. (Or else why would it exist at all?) So they don't. Instead, they accept what any letter says as true. Of course, they are free not to do so. But then the letter immediately loses its (institutional) logic as one of *reference*, and it becomes most difficult to recuperate it in terms of some other logic. (In my experience, a reader's skepticism about a recommended subject, whatever its cause, is usually rerouted to the author, who, presumably, wrote under the sway of some undeterminable motive; the text of recommendation, in other words, is always about *someone*.) Assuming the case where all conventions are in place, letters of application are processed as being true accounts.

Therefore, the text of recommendation is grounded upon a myth of presence: it is about a person, and it will produce a person. Even in our impeccably deconstructed times the letter of recommendation has not been deconstructed. Perhaps, as I've suggested at the outset, it cannot be, for if the person about whom any letter speaks cannot emerge from the words, what purpose would the text have? That it *is* a text I must trust I have already demonstrated. That it depends, more than most, upon a metaphysics of presence I will discuss most fully before I conclude. First, I want to treat certain consequences of the fact that any letter of recommendation is grounded in presence. Specifically, there are two: the text becomes embedded in a structure of duplicity, and it is governed, as a generic construct, by the reader rather than the writer.

The first of these features can be rather easily explained. The duplicity arises from the fact that, since the reader has no way to tell if the text is true, he or she nominally agrees to proceed as if it is true anyway. Of course, in this regard the reader is abetted both by the author and the institutional structure—no one has any interest in bringing into play the knowledge that all can be expected to have: no text is fundamentally "true" in the referential or empirical sense that the text of recommendation has been professionally empowered to have, and certainly not a text whose "truth conditions" only operate on the assumption that they are utterly unproblematical. This doesn't mean that the text of recommendation is false. Or that it can't be accurate (rather than, strictly, true) at another level of operation. Or any number of other possibilities. My point is that these other possibilities—ultimately, any other possibilities— have no theoretical privilege from the disciplinary framework within which the text of recommendation aims to have its consequence. Moreover, any other possibilities have of course no practical advantage.

Yet—again—a reader may choose not to accept the text as true. This is not the same thing as granting it some species of free play (fictional, tropological, etc.), as one does with virtually all other texts, or at least as one can do. Indeed, judging a letter of recommendation to be false is merely acting out the inverse of what the text proposes—and therefore insuring that truth remains its operative condition. If, earlier, I have implied that duplicity lies in reading the text of recommendation with a kind of willful unknowing that no more interesting, provocative things can be done with it than to accept what it says, my point here is that more duplicity lies in failing to realize that nothing is essentially changed when a letter of recommendation is dismissed out of hand. Why would one do so? I doubt whether anyone ever utterly does so. "I'm sorry, I'm terribly sorry," responds Emerson's son after *Invisible Man*'s narrator reads his letter. Then he states, after the subject declares he doesn't know what he's done, "But you must have done *something*" (Ellison, 188). Precisely. Whether for good or not—I must hope it's clear my example is ill so that the suspect nature of either effect can be clarified—*something* in the text of recommendation is always true.

The reader dictates what it is. The reason why the conventions through which the text of recommendation operate reside in the reader might first appear to be quite obvious: the purpose of the text is to make possible a verdict, and it is the reader who must make it, finally. Not all things follow, however, from the specific, practical aim of this text. The reasons why the reader enjoys authority in its conventions are very complex, and in part enact a structure of duplicity at a still deeper, more furtive level. I want to concentrate, first, on the presence of the author. Who is the author who writes the text of recommendation? The fabric of the text necessarily weaves an alternating pattern of disguise and disclosure. Little about the author's identity can be clarified, and so, as if by default, the reader is left to occupy a conventional vacuum in which ingenuities shade into disingenuities or professional imperatives override interpretive options.

Disingenuities? The author writes an analysis of a subject that is in fact a commendation. The fact that this is so obviously the case with any text of recommendation does not make it any less vulnerable to all sorts of embellishments or opinions, which are often quite difficult for a reader to understand because the kind of personal investment the author has made in them is not certain. Take the following statement: "X would be happier and of greater service to the profession if he were at an institution that had better students and better research facilities." Too gruff to be entirely commendatory? Certainly ingenious in the sense that what is meant is, the subject is too good for his present position. Yet possibly disingenuous if, on the contrary, what is meant is, the subject was never good enough to get out. Of course overall context provides some decisiveness about such reading alternatives. No convention provides enough; those applicable to the text of recommendation only lamely urge, I believe, that pluralizing a reading simply confuses the text, and risks making it useless.

Imperatives? Ostensibly about another, the text of recommendation is just as patently about the author. This fact cannot be acknowledged or perhaps even recognized in any conventional way. Does a well-written letter help a subject? What about one of some sort of unusual vividness? These questions are, I think, functions of one more basic about whether it matters for a reader to be somehow engaged by the convictions or the perspectives of an author for their own sake. A friend recently told me of reading a letter of recommendation by one of the most prominent critics in the country, who spent fully a third of the space propounding his own credentials. Should such a performance be held against the recommended subject? I don't think any conventional agreement is possible over such a question. What is possible is, again, the lame presumption that the author of a text of recommendation should ideally be an impersonal filter of facts and determinations.

This last point may be extended to indicate a final thing about the author who writes the text of recommendation: she or he may be so eminent that a reader may find it simply doesn't matter what the text says. Take the situation of a department's search committee that nominated a candidate to be interviewed largely because they were so impressed by the fame of the critic's very presence in the candidate's vita. What can be learned from such a case? The overwhelming importance of institutional power. Before its incarnation in one being, one personage, one eminence, textual conditions fall away as trivial affairs, frail and preciously "literary," rightly vulnerable to the grand resolve of elite standards, whose first law is that there *is* an elite. The text of recommendation is mandated to *impress*. (I've seen committees, on more than one occasion, talk about writing to a subject about an especially unimpressive, not to say critical, letter in a file.) There is a sense in which it doesn't matter how. There is certainly a level at which it doesn't even really matter if there's a text. Names alone can suffice. All that is required is that there are readers who can recognize them.

These readers are important because ultimately only they can answer, case by case, such typically complicitous questions as whether it's better for a subject to have an unexceptional letter of recommendation from a Name or an exceptional letter from someone who is not. Again, the text of recommendation is underwritten by the mythology of presence, and, as a mere text, abides in a conditional realm, sometimes no more than the act of the personage who signs it. This is why, especially if it is not, the text must always be taken possession of by the person who reads it. Only a reader is consigned the position of hopefully recuperating the indispensable vagaries of the author's identity, and only a reader is crucially positioned as being the only person who could activate the standardized form of the text. I have earlier considered its format, rhetoric, and hierarchical dispositions. I have not sufficiently stressed how all these things are the rather fateful product of instrumental, academic, bureaucratized language. This language constitutes, perhaps, the most crucial expression of a letter of recommendation as an acknowledgment of someone who is absent, thereby insuring how necessary is the presence of a reader on whom falls the decisive interpretive authority. In fact the language of the text has the character of a code meant to be deciphered.

The codified character that adheres, I think, to any sort of letter of recommendation was explained to me in its purest form by a woman who spent some years as a department head at a prep school. Over these years she wrote hundreds, if not thousands, of letters of recommendation for students, developing an elaborate, circumspect, and transparently formulaic processing system. That John was "brilliant," for example, meant that he was farfetched, or that his ideas were "carefully formulated" indicated that they were tepid. His "wonderful, outgoing social skills" in fact converted into his stupidity—and so on. What the woman did not explain to me is how she trusted that readers of these letters knew how to interpret them correctly. She just did.

Could she do so because her institution belonged to a relatively small class, which, taken together with its not substantially larger number of elite client colleges, comprised what could be termed an interpretive community? The whole profession of English, in any case, comprises no such community regarding letters of recommendation, even at their most apparently codified, and of course a letter about faculty rather than students has still more divergent, strenuous demands to address. Are they finally impossible to adjudicate? Certainly I have been tracing the profile of a profession where duplicity is the consequence of trying to arbitrate between conceptual divisions and where the job of negotiating among occupational levels can only be accomplished with more conscious rhetorical discomfort.

The text of recommendation has no theoretical sanction *as* a text, and enjoys an occupational sanction only to the extent it can be used to enable a verdict. This "extent" can't be defined—and if it could be, only then, curiously, would the letter of recommendation command textual interest. As it is, this text appears to be one of the things that makes the profession possible; there can be no debate about the need for letters of recommendation.[10] Therefore, I have been arguing that what is the case with these letters is more a matter of complacencies than conventions. We have at least a state of affairs where practice must be kept apart from theory until the moment of reading such a text is enacted at the personal, confidential level, whereupon there is just enough convergence to get the job done and enable the proceedings to continue, each time, toward their inexorable verdict. The system that situates the reader at the center where the text of recommendation will be made good must leave him or her without any clear, specific, rule-governed interpretive operations about what can be expected to constitute a valid reading.

There are times, in other words, when "thoroughly competent" means, well, "thoroughly competent," and not, say, "dull." But how to tell? Something termed "context"? In all cases? As if context itself was not a construction, even in the most standardized format? We are at least, presumably, well removed from the moment when the profession might have been able to devise a standard recommendory rhetoric (but how could this moment ever be retrieved, if it existed?) that functioned very much like a prep school code. I think of a story a former colleague, the product of another generation, told me of how his dissertation director had once written him a recommendation for a job he very much wanted. The director, wanting to cinch the case as much as he could, mentioned that my friend's mother lived nearby the desired institution and that my friend was very close to his mother. Only much later (and through a series of events too complicated to detail) did he find out why he didn't get the job: the department chair concluded he was homosexual. We may laugh. Yet who can guarantee that such interpretations do not persist to this day, every day? I mentioned the rare, dangerous formulation of "marital troubles" earlier. How many candidates for how many positions, we could well ask, are dismissed because letters of recommendation somehow suggest such troubles? And if the texts dare speak more openly of them? Conventions are always most urgently necessary when they have to function for texts that in some way depart from received modes of understanding. For such cases, the conventions applicable to texts of recommendation will not make them intelligible, and, indeed, are pleased to leave the individual reader, as if by default, to make up his or her own mind.

Let me give a more extended example. I was lately a member of a group that had to judge a man who had one letter of recommendation that was briefly considered by all of us. I had opined that it was one of the best I'd ever read. Part of the last paragraph ran as follows: "X is a great master of the tutorial and an even greater master of revision. Nobody reads manuscripts more carefully or makes more pertinent comments about style and argument. [Students] will find in him a challenging and insatiable debater and a fierce but constructive shredder and rebuilder of their arguments and essays." What I especially liked here is the pointed comment (no blather about "great devotion to students") and the vividly phrased sense of the subject (for once not "enthusiastic" or "dynamic" but "fierce"). This is a text that took risks, and I bought them. This is the same text, however, which another member of the group disdained. The tutorial? A too special instance. A "shredder" of essays? A horror. "Is this the way to deal with arguments?" my colleague asked, and went on, without bringing in other portions of the text, to conjure up a specter of wild-eyed contentiousness that, to me, could not be further from what the text had in mind.

Of course who is to say? The truth can't be known, the truth can't be told, the truth can only be interpreted, and neither of us could engage conventional constraints that would rule out either of our readings as unacceptable or inappropriate. (Perhaps it should be emphasized that this was an occasion where the subject himself could not be summoned. It is given to few subjects to be able to appear off the page. Many more stay on the page and are dismissed there. The basic purpose of letters of recommendation is to enable the decision about who gets invited to an interview and who doesn't.) To me, my colleague had merely reversed what I might term the straightforward—if unusual and challenging—commendatory mode; I saw no warrant in the text for the damning-with-faint-praise technique. Yet who is to say which of us floundered more? The reader of the text of recommendation is usually located somewhere between having too many strategies and not enough.

There is a solution, and it is fully authorized by convention:

supplementation. If one letter of recommendation is problematic, there are others. None of them may satisfy the imperatives for a perfectly decisive, valid reading, but all of them ostensibly permit a requisite verdict to be rendered with some justice and reality. If letters aren't enabling there are transcripts, statements, or proposals by the subject and perhaps writing samples or publications among other textual phenomena. The text of recommendation, in fact, participates in a network of supplementation, as well as being one element in the network. Furthermore, perhaps more than any other textual document, this text lays bare the very structure of the profession as a regime of supplementation.

Discussing the necessity of guaranteeing proper socialization by elites for young professionals, Larson gives the following conclusion of a study: "Successful completion of a professional education is an objective measure of . . . technical and normative socialization, but its inadequacy seems to be implied by the characteristic tendency of professionals to rely on personal testimonials and recommendations" (Larson, *Rise*, 230). Recommendations, however, don't close the network. Not even interviews do, although of course interviews do provide for a solution into which the text of recommendation can dissolve. This text only divulges how at every point the network needs to be open to further proceedings, more supplements. (The common practice of having interviewers write up their observations—thereby transforming the interview into another text—is almost deserving of a separate essay.) The system continues through any one verdict, just as one's first job—the circumstance of employment being the one I've been assuming for my purposes—is but the occasion for more socialization, routinization, and textualization.

The text of recommendation, then, is a supplement in a mesh of supplements. I believe it possesses another distinctive feature that none of the other supplements have. It registers better than any others that which it and all the other supplementation is supplementary *to:* human presence. Consider the statement that infrequently appears in this text: "I have no direct knowledge of his capabilities." How fatal to the metaphysics upon which the text is founded! Not only are recommendations termed "letters" (as if to code them as communications emergent from the actual categories of human intercourse); they are letters of *reference*, and therefore referable back to actual relationships in the real world of material facts. (The very state of affairs awarded the first paragraph.) Moreover, letters of reference are fraught with the compromised, indeterminate textual conditions I have been discussing because these have been purchased with a metaphysical warrant that can be claimed for no text: it can deliver flesh and blood.

Therefore possibly nothing is more moving about certain texts of recommendation than when they strain against the realization that they can't, after all, produce a human being, only a promise of one; the real must admit to being only a representation after all. Most have standard gestures that inscribe the strain rather than write it out; I am thinking particularly of conclusions that vary the injunction to "contact me if you have further questions." Yet by the end, many other letters unfurl a common stock of superlatives—"outstanding," "extraordinary," "splendid," "exceptional," "remarkable"—that push against the same sort of absence. My prep school woman, secure in her codes, could recall two occasions especially when they failed. In one, she wanted to write, "Whatever you do, take this one," and couldn't. In the other, she offered to come over to the college herself to insure acceptance. These more extreme cases dramatize how the absence to which the text refers can't ever be made present in the same terms, no matter how inescapable the fall into textuality is felt to be. One example of a phrasing I lately found particularly memorable is the following: "She is a pearl of great price, an asset not to be missed." I always find an air of sad resignation about such felicities. It is as if a voice is crying, "You should see her or know her as I do," if not, "Whatever you do, take this one." Alas, this is impossible. The words are only words. She may not be taken. She could be missed.

Some time ago the *New Yorker* ran a cartoon where Popeye stood before a personnel desk. Behind it was the personnel director, with the following outraged response to the paper in his hand: " 'I yam what I yam an' that's all I yam!' What the hell kind of resume is that?" It may be that the text of recommendation aspires to a position of impossible presence, wherein the words of another are converted into one's own, and then one's own words are made equivalent to one's body. If there is a narrative lodged in the text of recommendation, I believe it is this. (So many others—of teaching disvalued, research lost to the classroom, professional life broken into factions, personal life undone—simply never get on the page.) But this narrative never gets told: the subject is not quoted in the text, the body is never described. Since it can only be instead a professional narrative—by which I mean that, without the profession, there would be no occasion for any—presence has to be deferred, so that it can be subjected both to socialization and supplementation. This Popeye is, after all, a kind of savage who believes he is who he is and can be taken for who he declares himself to be.

I can't easily quote from what could be the best letter of recommendation I've ever read. I take it to be so because it bodies forth its subject so gleefully and enjoys its stylizations with such relish. The following is the most discreet example I can give:

> I've always thought of X's contribution as a year-round, day-in-day-out, seven days a week. But come to think of it, I rarely see [him] during the summer so maybe the best teacher I know of in the field just shuts down. I wouldn't have thought so much momentum, all that centrifugal power which swirls around him, which he pulls in from all allied fields, and pulls out of the upholstery of everyday

life, and reels in from the excited souls of his students—it never occurred to me that the summer would diminish a beat of that phenomenon. I know of similar powerhouses but they are all nuclear power plants which have shut down by the machinations of major government action. . . . Personally, I'm incapable of indifference in his company at any time or season. After fifteen years of exposure, you'd think maybe I'd be immune. But [his] influence is like influenza; he opens pores of learning in the most seasoned of academic tans.

Nothing I've maintained about reading letters of recommendation would make very much sense if this one is to everyone's taste. To mine the phrasing turns away from standard rhetoric so confidently as to constitute a rebuke to that rhetoric. It characterizes the figure of the teacher in conventional terms, although so powerfully that one can forget these terms are the givens of a disciplinary formation. Similarly, and finally, there is a vibrant human presence in this text, exactly because the text is so strongly *written*. It seems cynical to have to realize that he may not be whom he is attested to be.

I could state that this text concludes: "He is just terrific." It doesn't. Another I read does—almost as good. But the one from which I've quoted ought to. In a most fundamental way, all letters of recommendation ought to. More radically, they ought to state nothing else. In the best ones, one can see best how little else there is for all of them to say—beyond the circumspection and qualification, the hedging and the weighing. Or at least, if they can't say how terrific their subject is, they ought to be blank, for whatever else they do say because they can't say this is too fatuously truthful, too compromised with practicalities, and too ritualistic a participation in the supplementary regime that is the profession. Finally, in the text of recommendation, a highly estimable human presence begs to stand forth, worthy of the full consideration of the reader, if only she or he could see, listen, feel. "He is just terrific": it is a distillation of the utopian moment where it could be written of each of us that we are all, separately, wondrously available to each other—if only hapless advocacy, inexpressible fact, professional occasion, and utter presence did not all converge as appearing to be the same thing.

chapter two

WHOM TO ACKNOWLEDGE?

HAVE ACKNOWLEDGMENTS in books changed in recent years? Consider *Campus Life: Undergraduate Culture from the End of the Eighteenth Century to the Present* by Helen Lefkowitz. Her acknowledgments take up four pages. Three academic communities are named, four, eleven, and then thirty groups of people thanked, the staff at nearly thirty college and university archives recorded, diverse audiences for lectures recognized, five scholars who read the first draft considered, and finally assorted family, editors, and children are praised. Lefkowitz's book was published in 1987. What date would one want to set for an earlier time when such a lengthy, elaborate presentation of one's intellectual debts would not have been judged either proper or conventional? Whom would one have to acknowledge oneself to support such a speculation? And if there is indeed substance to it, what might be at stake in the change? Could the very nature of acknowledgment itself, and not merely the kinds of people, or institutions, have changed?

That there has been a change I am going to assume. Myra Jehlen's *American Incarnation* (1986) acknowledges twenty-nine people (and two fellowships). Her earlier *Class and Character in Faulkner's South* (1976) names fourteen people (and no fellowships). Another assumption however: there is no need to discuss the obvious fact that many books continue to set out their acknowledgments in ways that have changed very little over the course of several decades. Suresh Raval's *Metacriticism* (1981), for example, mentions nine teachers and colleagues as well as a summer of lectures at a school, reserves another paragraph for two particularly significant Bombay teachers, takes a third paragraph to record two other scholars, and then concludes with an administrative grant and a wife's devotion. This is the same sort of procedure that Philip Slater employs at the end of his preface to *The Glory of Hera: Greek Mythology and the Greek Family* (1968)—to go back no further—with the exception that Slater is even briefer, recognizing only one outstanding teacher and four colleagues. Both men give their acknowledgments at the conclusion of prefaces. There seems to be no special significance to this format. Evan Carton for *The Rhetoric of American Romance* (1985) has instead a separate page of acknowledgments but with the same sort of structure: the influential teacher, the colleagues, the financial assistance (Carton has both federal and local grants), and finally the family.

There may be, on the other hand, some significance to the fact that acknowledgments in the form of a compressed, sequential narrative seem to be far less frequent in the last couple decades. In *Neither Black nor White: Slavery and Race Relations in Brazil and the United States* (1971), Carl Degler takes some two and a half pages to describe very specifically the role over a dozen people have had in his project, and one can see just how it took shape with each one. In contrast, even when one does read some statement about how the book originated, as Juliet Flower MacCannell gives in *Figuring Lacan: Criticism and the Cultural Unconscious* (1986), it is likely to be just that, a "statement," followed by no more of a narrative than thanking the dean for time off, students for a germane course, and colleagues for kind words to other colleagues. But what significance precisely *does* one want to attach to this contrast, and, perhaps more importantly, just how many exceptions to it ought one try to note before either there ceases to be any contrast at all or there need to be so many qualifications that there may as well be no contrast? Of such problems is any study of acknowledgments fraught. There are either going to be too many examples or not enough. Either way, generalities are very difficult to manage.

And conventions are even more difficult to stipulate. Is there one, for example, that every book must have acknowledgments? James Twitchell's *Preposterous Violence: Fables of Aggression in Modern Culture* (1989) has none. What about the most venerable convention, that according gratitude and love to one's spouse? George Friedman in *The Political Philosophy of the Frankfurt School* (1981) can be read as strangely curt: "Finally, I thank my wife, Dorothy, who remained remarkably pleasant through the preparation of this book." Compare the fuller, not to say fulsome, words of Wayne Franklin in *Discoverers, Explorers, Settlers: The Diligent Writers of Early America* (1979): "I reserve my final thanks for Karin Franklin and our son Nathaniel, who have traveled with me across the literal American landscape and through the long journey of this book about other travelers. They know what it is that the words always leave out, and how many other things the working with words itself leaves undone." To contrast the two is inevitably to feel that Friedman has left out so much one wants to question what he had to begin with. Or was he merely impatient—even if the space for spousal acknowledgment abides as permitting more leisure?

The schema of an acknowledgment—ranking from general

to personal, and registering the intellectual or academic before the emotional or familial—is even elastic enough to accommodate some central dismissal, as individual temperaments often enact. "I have eliminated all the acknowledgements contained in the original essays," writes Clifford Geertz in *The Interpretation of Cultures* (1973). "Those who have helped me know that they have and how very much they have. I can only hope that by now they know that I know it too." (In his next collection of essays, *Local Knowledge* [1983], Geertz merely acknowledges where the essays were previously published.) An acknowledgment may be compared to a letter of recommendation, with three differences: (1) the acknowledgment is public, (2) it is purely dispensable from a reader's point of view to the book, which alone merits attention, and (3) it is indispensable only to those acknowledged, who can in theory be trusted to be content to remain anonymous. Or, if not anonymous exactly, then they can be entrusted to finer discriminations than those of public naming, as in this final note by Paul Smith from *Discerning the Subject* (1988): "Not wishing to be slaughtered on the bench of history—the fate of most women who find themselves mentioned in this slot of men's books—the person who has most affected (even effected) both this book and me during the time it took to write it forbids me to mention her by name." Smith's words suggest perhaps a final difference: unlike the subject of a letter of recommendation, that of an acknowledgment can be present while remaining absent by name, if only because the power of the "slot" has a conventional force which is inescapable.

I want now to inquire into the sources of this force by citing some remarks from the conclusion of the foreword to Stanley Cavell's *The Claim of Reason: Wittgenstein, Skepticism, Morality, and Tragedy* (1979). Cavell's acknowledgments could not be more in contrast to those of Geertz or Smith—and indeed, in their sheer zest, leisure, and pleasure more in contrast to most other acknowledgments of anyone else. So spirited is Cavell that he is at one point moved, after a list of names, to perform a sort of acknowledgment of acknowledgment, within which, he finds, lie more energies than acknowledgment itself can easily either accommodate or express:

> Such a list is something whose personal significance to me is quite out of proportion to its essential insignificance to strangers, and is thus at deliberate odds with the bright side of the intention to write.... What it suggests is that an elaboration of acknowledgement may declare a sense that complete acknowledgement is impossible, perhaps forbidden for one reason or another; and perhaps that one senses oneself for one reason or another to be insufficiently acknowledged.—If someone does not find such thoughts properly prefatory, I might offer instead the idea of a democratic equivalent of the Epistle Dedicatory, together with an aimless revival of the Epistle to the Reader.[1]

One could well think Cavell is at an end with these words. Instead, typically, he has four more paragraphs of acknowledgments.

Let me consider the first of Cavell's extremely provocative asides: what could be forbidden about the idea of complete acknowledgment? Is it implicit in the notion of any acknowledgment that it be incomplete? If my assumption is correct that today acknowledgments are more lengthy and complete, nevertheless what formal constraints continue to be operative? That there *is* form, or rather, formality, ought to be of course no less obvious than it is in Epistles Dedicatories. Consider only separation from prefaces. The moment when acknowledgments were accorded separate pagination from prefaces or forewords may prove to be as decisive for the history of acknowledgments as the moment when Epistles Dedicatories ceased to be commonly printed. Yet I don't think this separation itself constitutes form. Instead, it enables a more efficient, instrumental registration of what, beyond the merely personal need to recognize debts or express gratitude, acknowledgments are now burdened to address: namely, the fact of disciplinary specialization, which embodies, in turn, a whole host of questions about what a profession is, how it is organized, and what sort of relation it has with society at large. The answer proposed by any acknowledgment is clear: a *list*. Separate pagination facilitates listing, even as it permits, or indeed requires, more space for it. The result may appear relatively without style—an older narrative method, in comparison, begins to seem formal, not to say mannered—but this is only to further enable an accumulation of indebtedness that reveals how total are the demands for the publication of any book, and, most important of all, how eminently social. An acknowledgment of any completeness sketches a small society. (This is some of the fun of the Paul Theroux parody I quote from below in another context.) Whatever the subject of the book, it is, in the form of its acknowledgments, not so specialized that it lacks friends and spouses, casual occasions and public funding, affection and faith.

Do acknowledgments get longer as knowledge gets more specialized? Perhaps. Acknowledgments certainly get longer, I believe, as the social utility of specialized knowledge gets more marginal, even dubious, and at least suspect. What is knowledge *for*? It is as if the very autonomy necessary to maintain a professionalized discipline—its rules for access strictly controlled, its rewards hard to understand outside the discipline—gets represented in its acknowledgments as something, on the contrary, that is implicated in the most commonplace aspects of life. There is the most highly specialized intellectual activity and there is the lowly world in which it has to be implemented: both are embraced, equally acknowledged. In acknowledgments, the typing of the book shares space with its ideas or its organization. The "this list would not be complete" strategy includes not only the typist but proofreaders and copyreaders, and, if only for a moment, those who helped with the index as well as those who helped with the children appear to be as crucial as the former professors who made good their distinction or the present colleagues who never failed to be a source of stimulation. Everything is all of a piece and everyone fits. Acknowledgments, in sum, constitute the consolingly *democratic* gesture whereby the book, no matter how scholarly, demonstrates its accountability as a social product.

Far from dealing in the forbidden, acknowledgments are licensed to inscribe fundamental tenets of social mythology; knowledge, in its origins anyway, is collective after all, and implicitly honors itself to continue to be so in honoring those others who have helped make it what it is. Therefore, the idea of complete acknowledgment is forbidden because what would have to be recognized if the process were carried far enough would be the limits of the mythology. Books, after all, trade on their own energies. Not only are these impersonal and exclusive; perhaps they are finally disdainful of social purpose. The energies also arise out of conflict, some of it quite personal, or commonplace in the worst sense. If acknowledgments have indeed gotten longer, I believe it was inevitable that someone such as Martha Banta, in her own to *Imaging American Women: Idea and Ideals in Cultural History* (1987), would be moved to write the following: "Someday it would be fun if someone would extend the scope of the literary genre of the Acknowledgements section to include the names of everyone who proved an obstacle to one's project." (Has someone? If so, most likely a biographer, who is more dependent upon other people in highly specific and significant ways than most other writers are. Or maybe the author of a revised dissertation, although anyone who insisted upon repudiating a wretched Ph.D. adviser must first have been someone who had an especially intricate time getting the manuscript accepted for publication.) It might be fun to so extend the scope; it would be transgressive. The "scope" of an acknowledgment extends only so far because within its boundaries *no one* was an obstacle. The dean came through with released time as well as a grant, the typist didn't botch so much as a page. Furthermore, the application for a year at a prestigious institute was always successful, and its fellows were more stimulating than one's colleagues back home, none of whom were forgotten nonetheless.

Few are fortunate enough to be able to record the impressive story of affiliation and patronage acknowledged by E. D. Hirsch in *Cultural Literacy: What Every American Needs to Know* (1987). His project proceeds from top journals and preeminent professional organizations through NEH support and a year at the Center for Advanced Study in Behavioral Science to a letter from the Exxon Education Foundation. Just as happily, he has enjoyed the "greatest impetus" of a Valued Colleague; "without Professor Ravitch's original suggestions," and continuing support, Hirsch writes, "I might not have undertaken the book at all." How many readers of Hirsch's acknowledgments read them out of experiences in which they couldn't even get the initial magazine article published? How many will get no nearer to the Exxon Corporation than a gas pump? There may be some readers who take his narrative as a bitter rebuke, others who take it as an impossible encouragement for their own textual efforts. In the terms by which I've been discussing acknowledgments, Hirsch's possess—if not offer—an affirmation almost ritualistic in their force: the project can be seen through, there will always be those who recognize that it matters, and so on. Moreover, there is at least one radiant example of a work that finally opens out onto the highest reaches of American society. Hirsch, in sum, has written a superb acknowledgments—among the finest, in my opinion, in recent years. Banta speaks of "genre." Hirsch reveals that acknowledgments represent the genre of pastoral, not only in the more popularly understood sense of mixing high and low but in William Empson's sense (just to acknowledge him) of giving complexity the form of ideal simplification. Hirsch doesn't tell us if he had any obstacles; we don't want him to tell us. For there to be any "fun" at all (Banta again) it is essential that some things be forbidden.

Of course one could find that in acknowledging as much as

he does, Hirsch already acknowledges too completely. Knowledge in the scene of acknowledgment is ideally set within the warm glow of an intimate conversation. It is a wholly human thing. It is not a commodity. And yet there is everywhere in acknowledgments today the disclosure that knowledge is, precisely, a commodity. The time off or the year away is each as valuable as a grant, even if the grant more explicitly provides money, or rather time in the form of money. These things are all gratefully cherished. However, the cherishing becomes a blunter thing, and itself the more obvious consequence of a capitalistic economy, once large government and corporate agencies have to be mentioned, as they so increasingly must be for the book to have gotten written at all. There is a difference between the Center for Advanced Study in Behavioral Science and Exxon, and there is a linkage. Which is it in the interests of the social mythology expressed by an acknowledgment to recognize, the difference or the linkage? We might recall that (according to the *OED*) a later meaning of what it meant to "acknowledge" came to be "to own as genuine, or avow in legal form." (There is an example from the *Pinkerton Guide to Administration*, 1870: "A release should be acknowledged before proper authority, and recorded in the office for recording deeds.") We might speculate that today this later meaning has come to predominate in acknowledgments—no longer only, or primarily, personal confessions or admissions and instead at least just as often legalistic testimonies or certifications.

In this legal sense, precisely what is being avowed? That you don't acquire the capital necessary to produce anything unless you are embedded in the institutions that structure intellectual work?[2] There would seem to be nothing in the more comprehensive acknowledgments of the present to forbid either the disclosure about being so embedded or the gratitude about being so favored. And yet one could well wonder whether such disclosures push against the very constraints implicit in what Cavell calls "the bright side of the intention to write," as acknowledgments attest to it. What about, on the darker side, someone who writes in order to make money or to get promoted or to get more powerful? Acknowledgments of course are not mandated to adjudicate between sides. Once questions are raised—once they have to be present because the institutional setting in which scholarship is conducted cannot very well be absent—a whole world of unequal opportunities and ideological positions comes with them, and the scene of acknowledgment threatens to be too complicated for pastoral. Reading the most lavishly endowed acknowledgments, one can be reminded of Oliver North's definition of his Iran-Contra practice: a "separate, free-standing, full service operation." Of course it was not. It was only in the interest of a more dominant government practice that it be made to appear so. Similarly, the too-completely presented acknowledgments risk the specter of a book that was ultimately produced elsewhere and an author who is not completely the master of his or her own product.

Elsewhere: increasingly, it seems to me, the scene of acknowledgment has either shifted to somewhere else or become the result of a displacement from anxieties about authority located somewhere else. Where? It remains forbidden to say. Acknowledgments continue to present the indebtedness of a single individual, securely at the center of his or her authority, even at a time when, according to the poststructuralist or even postmodern critique, the author is either "dead" or so vitiated by various discourses as to be simply an "effect" of them. How has such a critique affected scholarly conceptions of what an author is or what sort of authority an author actually has? Is it too idle to speculate that some effect from the most sophisticated contemporary definitions is one reason why acknowledgments have grown longer—a form no longer quite sure where it begins or ends? These days we can at least certainly understand why this form traditionally or conventionally reserves the naming of parents or spouse and children for last: personal origin is thereby assured once more for a book. Perhaps it is accidental that Helen Lefkowitz, with whose book I began, begins by naming her husband first before the pages of testimony begin to mount.

Acknowledgments, as I have been discussing them, have been obliged to resolve two additional tensions that may be more strictly internal to a wholly academic economy of authorship: that between the personal and the professional, and between teaching and research. From the evidence of today's acknowledgments, the latter is the more worrisome. (The former appears as continuous as ever. Lefkowitz, for example, writes that "research assistance comes from the most unlikely sources"—and then cites her father-in-law. So it goes. In the domestic setting of an acknowledgment there is no discord. An especially elegant conciliation can be found in *The Building of Uncle Tom's Cabin* [1977] where Bruce Kirkham thanks his wife for permitting him to have another woman in his life.) Students are routinely thanked now, classes on the book's subject named. Of course they are all uniformly valuable; from the perspective of acknowledgments, no teaching ever dulled a subject or used it up, even if one may suspect that such repeated certification of the continuity between teaching and research is implicated in a larger regime of institutional indebtedness. Colleagues write recommendations for both students and themselves and request that recommendations be written for them. Everybody is urged to keep copies— or make duplicates—of observations, memoranda, requests. Common wisdom is that you have to "cover" yourself; someone else is certainly covering you. In the context of such interconnectedness, all remorselessly textualized, a more encompassing notion of agency may be emerging, best exemplified by how teaching has been situated in the acknowledged production of books. Publishing a book can be seen as a bureaucratic as well as an intellectual activity; you have to know how—and where—to write for a grant. Just so, writing a book bids to become equally an affair of departmental politics as well as institutional favor; you have to know how to teach the book you want to write, and therefore how to get the right teaching situation.

Articles often disclose this last continuity better than books—and of course one notices the practice of acknowledgments accompanying articles rapidly becoming commonplace. An excellent example is provided by S. P. Mohanty at the conclusion of his long piece, "Us and Them: On the Philosophical Bases of Political Criticism." Mohanty first mentions that most of the work for the article was done during the year he held a faculty fellowship at the Cornell Society for the Humanities. He thanks the acting director. He thanks three colleagues. Then he thanks four members of his seminar. There is another recognition: "I conceived the last section in its present form after a long discussion with Shekhar Pradhan one sunny afternoon in Oberlin, Ohio." (The generic overdetermination of pastoral may be noted here in passing. Whether it was in fact sunny, the "bright side" of intention admits the sun anyway.) And finally, after more thanks to four university audiences, there is this sentence: "Needless to say, all errors, excesses, eccentricities are mine own."[3] But if it is needless, why does Mohanty write this? It is as if there might be some danger that the authority for his text is not his.

And indeed, a text such as Mohanty's chooses to pay tribute to just enough of the external conditions of its own possibility that these conditions threaten to become its most internal realization. Mohanty's author is no longer sovereign but instead crowded out of his most originary impulses, where these have been transformed into things almost untraceable because they are the product of so many occasions. Those of day-to-day teaching, in terms of a customary schedule, are nonetheless fraught, I believe, with similar interest, even if the special circumstance of a prestigious fellowship somewhere else is more obviously a sort of thing to see explicitly acknowledged. We may ask in any case: when does a writing begin? What are its origins? How many origins can be represented in the writing itself? Or need to be? We may well be reminded of another of Cavell's attentions, "perhaps that one senses oneself for one reason or another to be insufficiently acknowledged." I want now to turn to this last, only apparently paradoxical point, by way of another fully orchestrated, book-length acknowledgment.

I want to contrast it to Lawrence Levine's *Highbrow/Lowbrow: The Emergence of Cultural Hierarchy in America* (1988), an impressively acknowledged volume typical of how academic knowledge is produced at the present time. Levine displays, besides released time, two years' worth of a Woodrow Wilson, the Massey lectures at Harvard, lectures and seminars at fourteen institutions, the Library of Congress staff, thirty-nine friends and colleagues, seven graduate students, and some twenty-seven others (including hosts, editors, and wife) who have given various kinds of support. However, Marianne Hirsch's *The Mother/Daughter Plot: Narrative, Psychoanalysis, Feminism* (1989) offers acknowledgments even longer (four pages), rarer, and far more compelling both in the use she makes of it and in its totality of detail. Hirsch gives both a junior faculty fellowship and a senior grant, a year's grant from a research center (including a seminar), another year's grant from an institute (twelve individuals are thanked), two women's groups (occasioning the recognition of eleven and eight individuals, respectively), seventeen colleagues from her home institution, another in a team-taught course (students unmentioned by name although "every one of them has contributed to this book"), ten others (for "bibliographic help" as well as "inspiring examples"), five more for research, unnamed others at four day care centers and another (named) for her household help, three children, three other members of the "extended family," the man who "shares the work of parenting with me," and finally both the author's own mother and mother-in-law.

What to say? Has Hirsch, almost despite her strenuous presentation of the most theoretically inflected feminism, unthinkingly relaxed into the secure stereotype of a woman's sensitive, caring nature? Certainly her book is a representative of a species that represents itself in its acknowledgments as almost more a life than a text. Furthermore, even if the point of Hirsch's acknowledgments is that there was no choice to make (the book of her life being convertible into the life of her book), a reader may nonetheless stare in wonderment at the rich mixture of all that a book asks of an author's life and all that her life gives to a book. There will be readers of such a book who would wish, I think, that they had not been told so much, as if they had been told a forbidden excess. There will even more certainly be readers who will realize, perhaps once more, that such acknowledgments as Hirsch's are simply inconceivable without the theory of contemporary feminism—of course in another register hers is a licensed luxuriance of subjectivity—and who may then wonder if such acknowledgments as Levine's were not somehow influenced by feminist theory. Indeed, feminism may be an additional reason that acknowledgments have gotten longer. It is more discernably one reason that acknowledgments are different in nature—more intimate (at least as a conventional option) and more self-conscious (as with Smith, cited earlier). In *Sensational Designs* (1985), Jane Tompkins thanks Stanley Fish for washing the dishes.

I want to maintain that Hirsch's acknowledgments are unprecedented in their completeness, and yet, for all that, they are not complete. Of what would complete acknowledgments consist? Not more household help named, nor more students. It would consist, I believe, in some acknowledgment of its own incompleteness, which is the one thing (maybe the only one) that Hirsch does not acknowledge. Her overwhelming record of support, affiliation, continuity, and interdependence of every kind enables the interpretation that it is nevertheless impossible to acknowledge everything completely. By this I don't mean, for example, that she mentions no obstacles. (Although someone who claims that every student contributed to a book might be said to have a sense of assistance so generous that obstacles could be difficult to recognize.)[4] What, after all, does it mean to acknowledge something? The more completely defined the something, the more the question changes from one of testimony on behalf of others into confession about oneself; Hirsch takes on so much to acknowledge that ultimately, if she is not explicitly expressing her gratitude for her own experience, she has at least not taken such a logic into account, as one internal to the very structure of acknowledgments, as Cavell suggests. Consequently, her acknowledgments emerge as an alternative formal license for self-acknowledgment. What it means to acknowledge something appears partially to be that we are not sufficiently acknowledged, or perhaps that there is so much of something else that we are temporarily in danger of losing the conviction of ourselves; writ very large, Hirsch's acknowledgments are Mohanty's but without his last sentence.

Of course this sort of problematic duplicity about authority is more familiar to us in creative rather than scholarly writing. And yet, just as with any writing, the scholarly text is about boundaries, even if the fact is more conventionally understood from the creative side. What is Eliot's "The Waste Land," we recall, but a text which, with its footnotes, aims to confound categories as well as extend the idea of what it means to acknowledge something—not to say an entire cultural heritage—in a mode of haunted, personal appropriation? The contemporary practice of acknowledgments I have taken to be most fully represented by Hirsch can be set alongside the preface written by Jeffrey Cartwright, the fictional biographer of a child-genius author in Steven Millhauser's *Pale Fire*–like novel *Edwin Mullhouse* (1972). "I have studied them carefully," writes Millhauser's Cartwright, "those smug adult prefaces. With fat smiles of gratitude, fit thanks are given for services rendered and kindnesses bestowed. Long lists of names are given cleverly paraded in order to assure you that the author has excellent connections and a loving heart." Cartwright will have none of this. He does his own typing. Edwin's parents were no help. "And so, in conclusion, I feel that grateful thanks are due to myself, without whose kind encouragement and constant interest I could never have completed my task; to myself, for my valuable assistance in a number of points; to myself, for doing all the dirty work; and above all to myself, whose patience, understanding, and usefulness as a key-eye-witness can never be adequately repaid."

So situated, Hirsch's acknowledgments should of course not be too strictly taken as the sort of thing about which Millhauser is writing a parody. Nor would my point be that Hirsch's acknowledgments are actually more a parody of Millhauser, no matter how unwittingly. The most interesting thing is that both Hirsch and Millhauser are engaged in the same kind of mental activity, which each respectively presents as mutually exclusive of the other. In this, each reproduces the cultural discourse about the difference between scholarly and creative writing, whereby the latter can be careless of the very social ethics about which the former must be so attentive. Partly the difference between Hirsch and Millhauser is the difference of the respective conventions in which each is located. The rest of the difference is merely that Hirsch has chosen a different form of self-presentation than that of fiction—which is not to say that her text is completely free of the vanity, resentment, and arrogance that Millhauser so gleefully sports (and that Banta, for one other, might willingly flourish, if acknowledgments could be extended in order to see the "fun").

By Hirsch's "text" I mean primarily the acknowledgments. Yet it is a curious feature of the rest of her book that it continues, next, with a long introductory chapter in which the schema of the acknowledgments is fleshed out in the form of what Hirsch refers to several times as a "narrative." Although principally in the service of her professional activities and what they reveal about how women's studies fare in the academy, this narrative has many sentences such as the following, about one of her articles: "I consider the writing of this essay a crucial moment in my thinking about mothers, daughters, and narrative."[5] Out of context, such a statement could easily be one from an autobiography, and, as it is, the writing possess little of the self-effacing scholarly manner. In fact Hirsch's text, particularly in its introductory chapter, *is* an autobiography that reigns in just enough of its most personal energies to pass as both literary criticism and psychoanalytic theory. (It is also a displaced memoir. The penultimate sentence of the introduction reads as follows: "Finally, this book is, in ways I cannot articulate directly, about my mother" [Hirsch, 27].) For this reason, however, its acknowledgments are especially unsatisfying, or rather unconvincing, and it is tempting to imagine that Hirsch wrote her introduction in order to try to redeem what was self-serving in them—only to produce a longer and more elaborate textualization of the same unacknowledged selfhood. I don't mean this as a criticism of Hirsch's study. (It is never more suggestive than in the matter of which voice—a mother's or daughter's—a woman writes in, and much of the nature of the double voicing I have been tracing stems from the book's very subject.) I do mean her study to be a sort of object lesson of what happens in a scholarly book when the thrust toward complete acknowledgment is so powerful.

What happens is hapless fiction. Acknowledgments, after all, are presumably "outside" the book, the "text proper." With Hirsch they are inside. Indeed, it is no longer clear on what basis we can tell the difference between outside and inside. It may be clearer to contemplate a book that is all acknowledgment (rather as *Edwin Mullhouse* is all self-acknowledgment). Or perhaps we could consider a story that is a narrative of acknowledgments, completely. (See Paul Theroux's acknowledgments in *World's End and Other Stories* [1980]. Something of its tone is indicated by the following example: "To Mrs. Annabell Frampton, of the British Rail ticket office, Axminster, my sincere thanks for being so generous with a temporarily embarrassed researcher; and to Dame Marina Pensel-Cripps, casually met on the 10:24 to London, but fondly remembered.")[6] The unspeakable moment in the acknowledgments is already the moment of fiction—the authorial self no longer exclusively turned inside out, but (re)turned just far enough back in to consider its own devices, and then only rarely (as Cavell) to acknowledge them as such, trying to keep a balance between generosity to others and fidelity to oneself. Would it be not more accurate to say that every moment in the acknowledgments is incipiently fictional (we recall Mohanty's sunny afternoon) and that the trick in writing them is to try to write a superior fiction?

What I mean by this can be indicated very simply by the last two sentences of Joseph Blotner's acknowledgments at the end of the second volume of his mammoth biography, *Faulkner* (1974). Few authors are likely to have accumulated the literally *hundreds* of human debts that Blotner gives in over four closely packed pages of reduced type. He concludes with the following statement: "My last statement of indebtedness is to those who have read this far and not found their names in the list when they should have been there. To them my apologies along with my gratitudes." Of course there may be no end of vanity behind such a statement. But the fine thing is that Blotner, overcome with the necessity for completeness, writes a space for incompleteness—and then dedicates it to unnamed others, not himself. It is as if the truth of his acknowledgments cannot ultimately be told, and, furthermore, that it would only be false if Blotner limited himself to telling what he can in the language of fact. So instead he makes up another truth of error and omission. It is of course an apparently simple gesture. I must hope that, precisely for this reason, it pointedly contrasts with the impossible completeness of more current practice that writes, and then writes some more, out of an indebtedness taken to be legalistic in nature and factual in scope. Acknowledgments, however, contain more truths than legalism can contain. And their factual record can be a sanction for self-indulgence—just as potentially comic as the Academy Award winner who, in acceptance, long-windedly winds down to ". . . and my mother."

It has been a premise of this discussion that the "genre" of acknowledgments is subject to social and cultural determinations, just as any other genre. There may be less awareness about this because the peculiar mediation among various institutional or political discourses that acknowledgments perform can only function if the pressures concerning how sovereign a project writing a book ought to be or how equal the opportunities for publishing one are not themselves acknowledged. Acknowledgments are nonetheless shaped by the larger need for mediation, which is arguably more urgent now when writing is representable as a sort of management of resources or publishing as a species of disciplinary transaction. As Michel Foucault remarked in a 1980 interview, in which he chose to remain anonymous, "anybody who writes exerts a disturbing power upon which one must try to place limitations."[7] Acknowledgments are one of those limitations. Virtually all nonfictional texts of all kinds present themselves to us as *embedded* things, and it is the job of acknowledgments to sort out the systemization, scale down the extrapersonal forces, put the brightest face on the textual project, and provide each of these faces with a human interconnection as well as a name. It is especially the job of acknowledgments to accomplish all this when it has gotten more difficult to do because so many books are each the product of so many debts that they are almost unlocatable from the site of individual authorship.

Foucault makes another statement in the interview: "A name makes reading too easy" (Foucault, *Politics*, 324). (The editor of the volume thanks, among others, two proofreaders and two foreign publishers for the use of the jacket design.) But how easy is too easy? Acknowledgments, which normally precede the text proper, introduce a reader into a specified human narrative. These days it may be so interdependent as to be oppressive. No matter, assure acknowledgments. Everything fits. There is no book that cannot offer itself as publicly accountable either for its intellectual occasions or as its own source on the basis of these occasions. It remains easy to receive such a book when the egotism that gave it rise is socially circumscribed, and when the possibly unwarranted energies that might issue from its pages have been introduced under the auspices of a human community that can be individually named.

Is writing dangerous because of its egotism or its unclassified energies? Is it less dangerous now if its egotism appears baffled or its energies too bureaucratized? A study of acknowledgments is necessarily a study in the dangers of writing—the negations it can give to social pieties, the "darker" intentions it can make prominent. How these dangers work themselves into the scene of acknowledgment, and are resolved there, is bound to remain highly speculative; if to study any writing is in part to study what it does not say, the study of acknowledgments is more hapless than most because the genre is only mandated to say a certain few things, and then in a socially proscribed way, according to conventionalized forms. This peculiar writing can be historicized; Toynbee's acknowledgments at the end of volume 10 of *A Study of History* (1954), for example, are not an example of the same sort of impulse to completeness—even at some thirty pages—which I have been treating. (Toynbee begins with Marcus Aurelius; he has the date when he saw his first Greek play; he knows how a Japanese puppet show he saw in Osaka in November 1929 helped him learn to write narrative; he even thanks God.) Toynbee is writing his intellectual history; ours is more circumscribed and academic—which is one reason why, forty years later, Toynbee appears so monstrously and inexplicably self-assured. Yet merely because acknowledgments can be historicized does not mean that the need for names has been any less taken for granted, however one might want to explain the need in terms of any particular time.

Finally, indeed, the most enduring feature of acknowledgments could be that they must abide as something *taken for granted*. Whether we read or write ourselves, we know what to expect as well as what is expected of us, when we acknowledge. A Cavell can enact subtle discriminations with the venerable formulas. He concludes his acknowledgments to *Must We Mean What We Say? A Book of Essays* (1968) in the following manner: "That I am alone liable for the opacities and the crudities which defeat what I wanted to say, is a miserably simple fact. What is problematic is the expense borne by those who have tried to correct them, and to comfort the pain of correcting them." What is "problematic," normally precisely what we don't want to hear about, is expressed so elegantly here, and with such care, that one can only find, I think, that the expected sort of answer has only been raised to a higher, richer power; such a representation as Cavell's is a more delicate example of what I referred to earlier as the "fictional" moment in acknowledgments. It is easy to read such words as Cavell's and to feel a renewed realization about why the scene of acknowledgment is a scene of stability and transparency: a book—any book—must not have cost too much, and the human expense paid out for its imperfections must have been worth it.

When we read acknowledgments we are ultimately less interested in the author's intellectual history, much less institutional affiliation, than in his or her generational continuities. Of all the things we take for granted in acknowledgments the most important may be that the book is more than a personal thing, and that it, like its author, takes its place in larger human rhythms that embrace both past and future. Let me give as a final example Patrick Bratlinger's concluding thanks in *Bread and Circuses: Theories of Mass Culture as Social Decay* (1983): "I suppose I have them to thank [his three children, to whom the book is dedicated] for keeping me at work those evenings when what I wanted to watch was not what they were watching. And I can be even more thankful to them for another reason: someday they may read this book and understand why I wrote it for them." In a world of vast, politicized discourses it is consoling to consider still another book that has to find its place as having issued from a comfortable domestic economy. And it is just as consoling, when knowledge appears to accumulate like so many debts that can barely be enumerated, that in fact what is written follows like daughter from mother, or sons from father. It makes the same sort of sense, which is not presumptuous, and which only has to be acknowledged rather than justified or explained.

chapter three

LACK OF APPLICATION

Is THERE a more *dispensable* text in the profession of English than a letter of inquiry about a job? Or should it be called a "letter of application?" Neither, of course, is exactly the same. Both may include a vita, and may, more accurately, be called a "cover letter." You have to write something if you're interested in a job, even if you only write in order to include some sort of itemization of credentials that is in fact far more relevant and compelling. That what you write is variously designated discloses how ephemeral it may be. The trick is that you can never be sure if it will indeed be so regarded. What is the significance of such a letter?

I don't know how many I've read during twenty years in the profession as a member of departmental search committees. I don't care. I do care about the few that were good: carefully crafted, humanly weighed, interesting, candid. I never preserved a one. What I have kept, instead, are copies of application letters (as I'll call them) that I've written myself during these same years. They've changed. I've changed. Nevertheless, I haven't changed enough in the professional sense, I have to conclude, because otherwise I'd have been able to stop sending out at least one of these letters virtually every year during the past twenty. What I want to do in this chapter is to use some of these letters in order to study not so much getting out—my own personal case—as the *text* of getting out. I don't think it matters for this text if one has not been in one position as long as I have (although the fact that I have been undoubtedly lends my own text an unusual degree of depth and nuance). If one wants to go anywhere in the profession—up, down, or laterally—one simply has to write these letters.

And one always begins somewhere. "May I present a profile of myself and my qualifications?" I began, during my last year of graduate school. (Although I was never satisfied with this sentence's combination of submissiveness and directness, I retained it for a few years.) The sort of things it was expected of me to say about myself and the qualifications I might be expected to produce were all already mediated for me by the legitimating principles of the profession. It's not necessary to set these out. Part of the force of any profession's standards is that they don't have to be stipulated—only either confirmed or violated. At the beginning of Dos Passos's *The 42nd Parallel*, the first volume of his U.S.A. trilogy, there is a pathetically funny example when poor young Fainy tries to compose a letter of inquiry about an ad he's found for a newspaper job:

> DEAR SIR (MY DEAR SIR)
> or maybe GENTLEMEN,
> In applying for the position you offer in today's Sunday *Tribune* I want to apply (allow me to state) that I'm seventeen years old, no, nineteen, with several year's experience in the printing and publishing trades, ambitious and with

excellent knowledge and taste in the printing and publishing trades, [sic] [1]

It's no good. Fainy's head just gets more "muddled." Dos Passos doesn't give what letter he presumably writes in order to get an interview with the old fraud, Doc Bingham. We already know he can't get past the correct form of address for a respectable position. Such an example reveals that the text of application, no matter how apparently dispensable or ephemeral, is nonetheless a text, which is already embedded inside rules of discourse.

Furthermore, it is a text whose foremost feature may be that it depends upon a certain presentation of oneself. Fainy realizes that he has to expose a "profile," but he doesn't know this concept, and immediately he's haplessly enmeshed in the peculiar fusion of modesty and confidence required by the presentation. We may recall the *New Yorker* cartoon about Popeye, "I yam what I yam." In one sense the letter of application is possibly even more haunted than the letter of recommendation by the great dream of presence and self-coincidence; one applies in order to offer oneself precisely as one is. In another, far more telling sense, one's very first sentence reveals such a dream to be fatuous. It is never easy to know what to say and what not to say. It is impossible to get this exactly right, no matter how one chooses to efface oneself within formal conventions.

Or not efface oneself. One of the most interesting public moments for the profession of English in recent years, I believe, occurred during Stanley Fish's article for a 1988 issue of *PMLA* against its policy (one reason for its hegemony in the field) of "blind" submissions. Fish allows himself this aside: "As things stand now, for example, I am against blind submission because the fact that my name is attached to an article greatly increases its chances of getting accepted." [2] Of course Fish is not writing a letter of application. A Fish doesn't have to. If he once did, however, one may be sure he participated in the same subject position of anyone who ever has: he bestowed his pride at no small risk because he was nameless. The author of a letter of application is always nameless. She or he is imperiled to put down just enough of a self to serve as a foundation for a suprapersonal configuration of experience and commitments, publications and prospects. Only much later—if at all—does one get to concede a more narrow, unregenerate self that of course is not without vanity, anxiety, and ambition. In the text of application it is probably best always to be a strict formalist. Neither author nor audience is likely to be known to the other. Form possesses the additional advantage of being able to process the essentially meaningless dimension of such a communication.

But what is form? Even if letters of application finally have little significance in themselves, they do not exist at all apart from some textual constraints. Moreover, even if the self in these letters is no one—or no more than a "subject position"—he or she must still pose as someone in order to make contact at all. I want to insist upon these problematic matters because my own letters, virtually from the first, have always proceeded under the assumption that they matter more than they do, and, perhaps worse, that I am someone more distinctive than textual (not to say institutional) conditions allow me to be. Let me give at this point the penultimate letter—or rather, Letter—I evolved (sent to two English department heads in 1987), and then try to unpack its peculiar strategies. Or lack of them.

2

> *Is man a sort of novelist of himself who conceives the fanciful figure of a personage with its unreal occupations and then, for the sake of converting it into reality, does all the things he does—and becomes an engineer?*
> —*Malcolm Lowry*

Dear X:

One writes these letters to distinguish oneself. So I could begin by stating that I've lectured in seven countries, been awarded two Fulbrights in American literature, published about twenty articles, and next year, at last, expect to publish a book. But one writes these letters for all sorts of other reasons, and of course there abides through them the sort of thing my epigraph expresses (and that such letters as this seldom do). I should be content merely to say that I'd like to be considered for your position in American literature.

Why? I don't think this letter obliges me to say. Let me write this much anyway: I'm good. Or at least better than my present position, which I've occupied for too long. (Vice versa might be closer to the truth.) This past summer I happened upon a lovely distinction by Joe Greene, the Pittsburgh Steelers' tackle recently inducted into the Football Hall of Fame. "The game," Greene was speaking about, "that's the important thing—to play the game." And then he emphasized: "I didn't play defensive tackle. I played the game from the defensive tackle position." I've played the game and I love it. But I'd love it more and play it better if I had another position.

I may as well be candid because, if my knowledge of how hiring is done counts for anything, it is a human being you will ultimately decide to hire, not a record of achievement. I would of course like to impress myself upon you as precisely the sort of man you would prefer to have in your department. And yet, amid the din pressing in from everywhere (you may have already received more such letters than you can easily read), how to avoid ghostlier demarcations when I'd like to make keener sounds? I don't know how to do it. I suppose here I'm only trying to engage your sense of deeper resonances, richer nuances.

The enclosed vita will provide its own score. Is it a supplement to this letter or is this letter a supplement to the vita? Mine, I think, at least reveals me to be an experienced teacher of modern American literature, as well as an active contributor to its professional discourse in terms of conferences, publications, and awards. Perhaps my additional interests in literary theory, modern English literature, and, most recent of all, travel writing are also reflected there. What else? Little else, I believe. The enormous range of courses I've taught here, for example, is not disclosed, nor what it has cost me to summon into public view enough of a visible career upon which to lay claim to some distinction. The distinction is for you to judge. The career has never been one for me to simply, well, "engineer." I like the way the Emerson of "Circles" puts it: "For we live in several worlds, each truer than the one it encloses, and itself false in relation to the one that encompasses it." I've never quite been content, either professionally or personally, to occupy one world during nearly twenty years of teaching at one university, and in the past decade the trope of a different "world" has become a literal fact for me.

What else to emphasize but my need for what Emerson elsewhere terms our "due sphericity," which is insatiable? I would ask you to assume nothing more about me than that I can do whatever is required of me, do it well, and do it with a thoroughness that redefines the initial requirement. Here I've done everything in the department but act as chair. (In China I played on the department basketball team.) I think I am exactly the sort of teacher who *performs* his abilities, both inside and outside the classroom. In the end, it seems to me, it is the performance, and not, or not merely, the ability that you want. It has taken me a long time to realize my potential as a scholar, and now I'm bursting with ideas, projects, prospects. I've never been more confident of myself as a teacher. But even as I write these words, I smile at a reader in the image of Mae West, who once opined that she liked to date younger men because they had shorter stories; I must beg to be forgiven for not providing a longer and more passionate paragraph on my whole life.

Recently I came across this lovely statement from Heraclitus: "The fairest order in the world is a heap of random sweepings." A decision to hire someone is, I believe, finally both a random thing as well as an affirmation of fair order. In the name of one if not both, I hope you'll consider me.

Sincerely,

3

It will be noticed, first of all, that I have an epigraph. I've never read a letter of application with one. I give one for anything of any consequence that I write, and I first began doing this for letters of application six years ago. The year before Lowry, I had the following from Chesterton: "Very few people in this world would care to listen to the real defense of their characters. The defense which belongs to the day of Judgment would make such damaging admissions, would clear away so many artificial virtues, would tell of such tragedies of weakness and failure, that a man would sooner be misunderstood and censured by the world than be exposed to that merciless eulogy." I believe I liked this one better. I've never been comfortable praising myself or urging myself upon anyone. I suppose, nevertheless, that I scrapped Chesterton after a year because my occasion, after all, was somewhat less than the Day of Judgment.

Why doesn't the text of application have an epigraph? Partly because this text is so grindingly formal, so *stupid*. It is as if the author is bid to put away his or her intelligence, or perhaps to reserve it for occasions which are not, somehow, social. This is dishonest, of course. Get past the application and into the interview room, and one will be ruthlessly judged not only on one's convictions as a teacher or knowledge of one's field but just as much (and who is to say not even more?) on whether one appears, say, either too ironic or not ironic enough. It might even matter if your shoes aren't shined. That is, one will be judged as a human being, rather than, well, an "engineer." Perhaps the rest of the reason that a text should not adorn itself with an epigraph is that otherwise it risks constituting itself too fully as something too personal, too fictional (as Lowry suggests), and this is to be feared, because the terms are bound to be elusive, maybe bewildering, and certainly difficult to respond to in a bureaucratic fashion.

I'll never know if 99 percent of the chairs who read such epigraphs threw the pages into wastebaskets before getting to the first paragraph. The 1 percent who didn't, or 10 percent, or *some* percent: these are the people to whom I imagined myself writing because these are the people for whom I felt I could distinguish myself, and do so immediately from the rest who would never dream of writing an epigraph. These others bothered me. Only in recent years did I come to acknowledge how much—hence the epigraphs. One I didn't use was a statement of Andrew Hacker's from an article on education: "As it happens, the mobility of teachers among colleges is at an all-time low." One I did for several years—only in the first paragraph—was Blake's injunction: "Bring out number, weight, and measure in a year of dearth." I suppose I meant to imply with Blake that it is always a year of dearth if there is only number and so on. I never fully acknowledged that for the text of application itself—mandated as it is to get right to the point and waste no space—each writing is always in a year of dearth, in which ironic framings or humorous perspectives are irrelevant.

So am I to conclude that all of mine were superfluous or fatal? I have a draft, undated, but probably from the mid-1970s, in which I quote the following "hint" I read somewhere from a personnel marketing firm: "The biggest mistake of most resumes is that they contain too much information that is not needed (which only works against you) and too little that is really germane to the employer's decision." This is a good example, I believe, of how the discourse of application, as enshrined in more handbooks than there may be jobs (although these handbooks have produced jobs for English teachers—one staple in most English department menus now being a course in business writing, in which students learn to write . . . letters of recommendation) transforms quality into quantity.

There is too much there, too little here. Always the model for the "employer" is that of a no-nonsense business executive whose time is precious and whose appetite for the bare facts is ravenous. At the conclusion of my first paragraph I say that I "should be content." But I've never been content before such a personage. However I may have been judged, the real problem with these epigraphs may have been that they disclose too much pride.

It appears to continue, more openly, in the first paragraph. Hence, it is difficult for me to describe how hard-won this paragraph was for me to write, how uncertain (at best) or craven (at worst) so many earlier initial paragraphs were. I never liked any of them. Should the first paragraph in this text merely set out the factual pretext for the more developed second, or should the first aim to be somehow arresting of itself? Standard guidelines for the application letter recommend the first option, my own inclinations argue for the second. Yet it took me years to settle on something. In a kind of perverse way, I always wanted to parody the more predictable, humble mode—until I came across the short text, "The Job Application," by the Swiss writer, Robert Walser. I couldn't better it. I did manage to resist the impulse to quote it. Walser's first two sentences to his "Esteemed Gentlemen" are as follows: "I am a poor, young, unemployed person in the business field, my name is Wenzel, I am seeking a suitable position, and I take the liberty of asking you nicely and politely, if perhaps in your airy, bright, amiable rooms such a position might be free. I know that your good firm is large, proud, old, and rich, thus I may yield to the pleasing supposition that a nice, easy, pretty little place would be available, into which, as into a kind of warm cubbyhole, I can slip."[3]

The ultimate reason why I could sound proud by 1987 is that I'd accumulated enough honors and publications. That is to say, enough of my work outside the classroom (a burial ground of aspiration, from the point of view of the text of application) had proliferated to constitute a *career*. What is a career?

There are of course many ways to define one, many combinations of conviction, ambition, and achievement, many ways to reproduce in oneself the successively generated series of expectations evolved out of one's profession. What I find interesting about my sense of a career is that at the center of it, as at the center of this first paragraph, is an absence: no book. Initially, I'd attempted in my text to transpose questions of quantity into those of quality. Then I had to acknowledge that differences of degree couldn't ultimately be separated from differences in kind, especially when I'd managed enough quantifiable success myself. Finally, here, in this first paragraph, I tried, in effect, to reverse the direction of my original transposition. But still no book.

Should I have mentioned this? Should I have assumed, as I did, that anyone who read my text would flip to the vita to check for a book? A career is not simply something we "have." It is something we construct. It may be that both the materials and the models are given to us by our profession. "To begin," writes Edward Said, "is first of all to know with what to begin."[4] So the profession tells us. Yet it doesn't tell us what story we should tell ourselves—what to stress, where to pause, how to make a transition, and, most important, what each individual should conclude about such moves. My lack of a book registers, I believe, the lack that is at least one constitutive element in any career. You may tell yourself you've done enough, achieved enough, been recognized enough. Nonetheless, what firm basis authorizes such a conclusion? Even a Fish, as he admits, still wants to be published again. Much of the ruthless formalism of the handbooks about letters of application is explained by the absence the rules strive to cover up, for to write a letter of application is always to be found wanting on some basis. (To use that of a book: if one, why not two, or why with this publisher rather than that, and why not more recent? And so on.) My procedure was simply to mark this basis—and to trust, perhaps, that some conceivable reader of my text could see that in a certain sense the mark was almost as good as the book.

Lack of Application | 59

My second paragraph, I think, is built around another assumption about this hypothetical reader: that he or she will recognize that I am someone not only capable of wit but of a certain, well, bravado. Application guidelines usually characterize the second paragraph as the one where the applicant explains why he is interested in the position and what she can do for the "employer." I choose to devote separate paragraphs to each of these, and, again, in the second, to address directly my dissatisfaction with my present position. But at too great a cost? With another quotation that this time might be read as frivolous? It is hard not to confess that with an analogy from sports I may have trusted my reader too unwisely. It is easier to consider here what might be at stake in making such an analogy in the first place.

At the limits of any discipline there are questions or relations that are hard to describe from within that discipline. The most acute for me is failure. Is it less possible in the discipline of English to describe what might constitute failure than success? I think so. Certainly the situation of someone such as me, who has been in one position long enough to be obliged somehow to negotiate the very fact when writing a letter of application for another position, discloses that I've had at least to consort with failure: I simply didn't accomplish all that was in me. Yet the discipline is not very secure about specific definitions—just as it is quite secure about how specifically success can be defined; the book one person may be blamed for not writing is not necessarily the same book that another person is praised for writing. Therefore the fact that I have to resort to another field of endeavor in order to provide some coherent measure of insufficiency testifies, I would claim, to the specter of failure that everybody in the profession has to live with, but in part only because nobody has any vocabulary for speaking publicly about it.

In a 1976 text I quote something I read about an exceptionally talented basketball player who never made it to the professional level: "He gave them something," the writer says of various NBA tryouts, "never all of what they wanted." My point was that what I've given in my present position is already more than what "they" want; I have more to give. Then I continue, defensively: "I'm aware that the world of professional basketball is not the world of higher education, but there are corresponding requirements for ability, and, more important, performance." (In fact I felt the two worlds to be disturbingly close. A few years before this a colleague and I developed a running joke about how college recruitment and staffing should be conducted along the lines of NBA draft and trade policies.) I still like this analogy. I think I dropped it the next year because I feared it was too candid.

From an undated draft is the football coach who said of his quarterback, "He's not a great runner, nor a great passer, but he's the kind of guy who gets things done." I never used this. Too corny—and far too labored in a letter of application to try to assert how departments of English need exactly these sorts of people. (Indeed, they may be more essential there—showing up at all meetings, volunteering for committees, even keeping the coffee fresh—than for football teams.) Or from a clipping comes the halfback who said, "The time to go down is when they bring you down—and if they don't bring you down, you don't go down." I never used this one either. Too close to being witless to be profound—and, in any case, melodramatic for my purposes, although I felt more accurately represented by this halfback than the quarterback. The careful distinction by Joe Greene abides for me in another dimension altogether. I still find it so sublime as to function as a rebuke of anyone who cultivates a specialization and forgets the wider energies that are its very reason for being.

Yet are they indeed? Does the discipline especially care whether the eighteenth-century specialist finds Pope merely the most enabling name with which to profess poetry? More to my point, does it care in which "league" the professing is getting done, or what larger interests are not getting served if all the right players aren't suiting up in the right uniforms?[5] Such vexing questions may only be the more vexed by my analogy, and if I return to the hypothetical reader I have no ready answer about what precise kind of response I expected. Like letters of recommendation, letters of application have a schema, but no interpretive conventions. (It could be argued that the schema is so crucial because the conventions are so empty.) Furthermore, again like letters of recommendation, letters of application give over all interpretive authority they could have to the individual reader. The scandal of anything unusual in the text is so great because the accuracy about how any reader may interpret it is so small. For all I know two department heads may have swooned over my Greene analogy. There are lots of other reasons why I didn't get interview offers anyway. That's the trouble with a text of application. There are always lots of other factors well off the page. It's just a text.

4

Notice that my letter is too long. A few earlier ones were longer still. "Too long (preferred length is one page)," states the first of "Ten Most Common Resume Mistakes" from a typical handbook. The fourth is the following: "Overwritten—information is scattered around the page—hard to follow." I never cared about any of these rules.

Indeed, in the light of their imperatives, it would be fruitless to consider the rest of my text. It raises the matter of its own genre, it quotes from Emerson to Mae West, it speculates, jokes, cajoles. Carefully self-absorbed, it could be read as strangely defensive or even more strangely contemptuous. If it's a compelling letter of application it only is because it's a compelling piece of *writing*—which is neither the point nor the occasion. It's almost as if I didn't care about either.

Does my text represent some sort of method then, or express some strategy? I think I can answer by referring to one of the five aspects of form that Kenneth Burke describes in

Counter-Statement. "Conventional form," Burke states, "involves to some degree the appeal of form *as form*. . . . Any sort can become conventional, and be sought for itself—whether it be as complex as the Greek tragedy or as compact as the sonnet."[6] What to say but that in my repeated writing and rewriting of the text of application I never demonstrated any real interest in the conventional form of this text? The irony (just to choose this word) is especially grim since the text of application *is* nothing else but conventional form. More generally, Burke defines form as "an arousing and fulfillment of desires. A work has form in so far as one part of it leads a reader to anticipate another part, to be gratified by the sequence" (Burke, 124). Such arousal there may be in my text, but it risks inhibition because it is not conventional, and thereby is too vulnerable to being understood as pointlessly complicated, inwardly elaborated, and severely mannered.

My text of application, in sum, is a good illustration of the limits of a text in dictating the terms of its own reception. These limits are not textual at all, but institutional. The authority for them lies with the reader not the writer. (That this is so wholly the case with a letter of application is one consequence of its form being so utterly conventional.) If every letter of application expresses some condition for its own rejection, mine only compounds the fact by generating more conditions—in trying so impossibly to close down every conceivable one; I am quite frank, for example, about the social consequences of being a member of a department, but in exhibiting this consciousness I can't consider whether someone reading the letter might actually want as a colleague the man who writes it. Indeed, this sort of consideration is ultimately not mine to make. The more mundane things may be more entirely out of any applicant's hands than the scholarly ones. It's as if I can't admit the elusiveness of anything mundane—which is the very category the happily conventional form of the letter of recommendation is pleased to leave to take care of itself.

One quotation I've always refrained from working into a letter of application is something that Lionel Trilling's tortured student, Tertan, says to the Dean in "Of This Time, Of That Place" about his Professor Howe. It's in a letter to the Dean—a sort of antiletter of recommendation—where Tertan attempts to explain how Howe both has and has not been a Paraclete. "To him more than another I give my gratitude," Tertan states, "with all respect to our Dean who reads this, a noble man, but merely dedicated, not consecrated."[7] I love this distinction as much, if not more, than Joe Greene's. *Consecrated*, precisely: that's what I've always wanted to be in the profession, what I've taken myself to be, and, more to my point here, what I've written myself as being on the solemn occasion of applying for a position. I may actually be or I may not. What it's taken me many years and many letters to realize is that such a conception is simply not what is desired, at least as given in a letter of application. Consecrated? It's too exalted. Consecrated? It may not even be desired off the page.

Similarly, the page is not going to function as a site of communication if too much awareness is demonstrated about how empty it is. For a number of years in my text, I used to have a second paragraph that ran thus: "A while ago I asked a woman who's had much administrative as well as editorial experience what precisely to say on letters of application for a position. Her advice was primarily negative: anything you say in such a letter doesn't really matter. She wasn't able to tell me what does." Easy to conclude now that it's better not to be problematical about what's so carelessly, or ceaselessly, conventional. But not if you take yourself to be consecrated and therefore shrink from the commonplace as if it were a desecration.

Another commonplace: the text of application is completely impersonal. This has only aroused in me the imperative—not a mere impulse—to saturate it with subjectivity. Why? Because, for so many years, this subjectivity was all I had? In one measure, yes. But my subjectivity remains all I have, even if it's been transfigured into as many books and articles as the work of Stanley Fish. In another measure, the conventional form of a letter of application has never stilled in me the desire to parody it. My favorite of a number of parodies of letters of application published some years ago in *Esquire* ("An M.F.A. grovels for work") was the one where a man writes to his father for a job listed in the MLA bulletin. I've never forgotten the letter John Berryman mentions in an interview that he once got: "Dear Mr. Berryman. Frankly I hope to be promoted from assistant professor to associate professor by writing a book about you. Are you willing to join me in this unworthy endeavor?" Berryman did. "I practically flew out to pour his drinks while he typed."[8] English department chairs, however, are not poets, and the profession leaves it entirely up to oneself whether one wants to drink while typing.

I have been recounting a narrative in which I've unremittingly tried to overcome with textuality the most banal of texts. The struggle was always unequal: no matter how I strained against it, there remained the same dumb, ordinary, impervious form. Within this narrative, however, is embedded another: the attempt to make the formal "gratification" Burke speaks of convertible into gratification about me. Not a textualized "me." Me as I actually am, or, I might say, me as Popeye presents himself to be in the cartoon, right there in front of the desk. Of course such an attempt is licensed by the convention of letters of application; what you want to display is your best face. Yet the effort is conceded to be lodged inescapably in a *text* for all that—and it is better (so the logic could be construed) to get the text over with as efficiently as possible so that a real flesh and blood contact can be made, if it is decided that it should be made. My text(ualizing) misses all this. Just as I had almost consciously drifted into blurring the difference between a mere position and a priestly calling, I had become haplessly trapped somewhere in the irrevocable gap between the word and the thing. I was aware no text can demonstrate a body. Yet my conspiracy against form left me no theoretical self-possession—and, in a sense, dispossessed me of what self-possession I was accorded in the conventional letter.

The only portion of my text of recommendation that I ever liked—that is, I think, *accepted*—was the last paragraph. According to the guidelines, this is the place where the applicant is free to "indicate your desire for a personal interview and your flexibility as to the time and place." That is, the text opens out into life. Or, to put it another way, the text confesses its feebleness as a text and begs to be reborn in another realm entirely. Alan Feldman has a lovely poem, "Plea," whose burbling caricature of a letter of recommendation is, to me, never more resonant than in its concluding lines, where the suppliant pledges

> That I will sincerely storm and range and rain and be a sea
> Of duty over breathless academic years when I expect to complete
> Nullification of my fingerprints and assume the radiance
> Of a billiard-ball flying from the stiff out-pointed finger
> Of your chairmanship, while my wife and first child
> (Whose conception awaits only your reply)
> Smile together in the yard of our long-awaited home.[9]

My own version of this was the conclusion of a letter I was gleeful to be able to write on University of Riyadh stationery in 1981 in the middle of my first Fulbright: "I do present a marvelous opportunity for a member of your department, or you, to fly over and interview me. But, alas, the Saudis wouldn't give you a visa. I could, however, be interviewed by phone; U.S. connections from here are excellent—so clear as to be local, except that the analogy is idle, since local calls here are so bad as to be transcontinental. Even in the guise of a fateful form letter, I'll look forward to your reply." I don't believe I ever got one. (I hadn't been able to resist quoting from the Koran: "Some are bound for the Fire, some are bound for the Garden, and Allah does not care.") But it was fun to imagine reaching out of the words so lightly. I didn't feel trapped by the text.

The life in the text, the text in the life: to write a text of application as long as I have is to feel, more accurately, perpetually stalled. The same things have to be said, and said in the same way. Meanwhile, the most important things still can't be said, only it gets more impossible to say them. Who first claimed that every career has five stages? The schema is as follows: (1) Who is X? (2) Get me X. (3) We need someone like X. (4) What we need is a young X. (5) Who is X? I believe that anyone who writes a letter of application, no matter at what chronological stage in his or her career, is in the position of the first stage. A career is recognition. One applies to some one, some other, in order to get it. The text of application discloses, however, that either one still doesn't have recognition or one has to begin all over again as if one didn't have any. But what is particularly interesting about this schema is how the second stage arises from the first: one does not ask, one is *asked for*.

This is to say: one is already present. This can of course be understood in an abstract, prototypical sense: if one doesn't get to be one's own model unless one is recognized, one doesn't get recognized unless one is one's own model. This wonderfully circular process can be implicated in textual terms. What may be even more compelling is what can't be so implicated— as the transition between first and second stage suggests. One is already present because one is known, specifically, individually, physically. Out of this knowledge one is called for: "Get me X." The process is familiar to everyone: a chain or network of people who know each other suddenly is responsible for how one of them comes to occupy a new position after it becomes vacant. It happens. It doesn't seem possible that it could for any one person who has to resort to a letter of application. Yet who can determine, especially if the letter is eventually made good as a job, that some sort of personal linkage had not been responsible for the actual hiring? Indeed, such a connection may be the crucial element in the great majority of hirings; common wisdom insists that the most important requirement for a job is to "know somebody." The text of application ideally dissolves in this manner into life, not only because it is meant to but because it is conventionally designed not to *coalesce* at too great remove from circumstances, personal loyalties, and friendly factions.

Therefore it appears to me to be self-destructive to keep rewriting a text whose very basis is to self-destruct. This is not to say I won't. The one I sent out last year (still barren of book) to two places I finally whittled down to one page, just as all the handbooks agree, and I managed to refrain from inscribing the fact that it had taken me some twenty years to achieve this mere page. Yet one always applies oneself, so to speak, from *elsewhere*. The trick is not to be confined to a text. The trick is to be outside it or, more ideally, already there. A letter of application, like a letter of recommendation, is a text of absence—or failed presence; it comes to the same thing. The difference from a letter of recommendation is that in a letter of application you have to write your own absence yourself.

Somebody says the following in Joyce's *Ulysses*: "And when all was said and done, the lies a fellow told about himself couldn't probably hold a proverbial candle to the wholesale whoppers other fellows coined about him."[10] This is only just. More crucially for the authorized professional, it's more favorable. Better to be recommended than to apply. Better still to be recognized, and then neither to have to be written nor to write. Applying is a comedy, and the lovely thrust of Feldman's poem is that you apply to someone in order to invite that person to conspire with you to attest to your absence. But I can't let go Heraclitus, much as I'd like to substitute Feldman. Heraclitus speaks to all who belong in better jobs, or don't deserve the better ones they've got, or won't get better luck, or have already gotten too much. Best of all to be random.

chapter four

CROAKING ABOUT COMP

THE OTHER DAY, I forget where, I read the following sentence: "Religion has a major impact on society." It's a comp sentence. It has that special witlessness, the true instinct for something, in Cynthia Ozick's phrase, "unerringly wrong."[1] I haven't taught composition for a year—after two sections each semester every year for nearly twenty—but I'll never forget what sort of sentence gets committed in English composition, even if I never teach it again. I hope I don't. I hate comp.

Not teaching it, I've become seriously interested in composition theory—and the first thing that interests me is almost the last thing: why the sheer detestation for teaching this subject on the freshman level never seems to get expressed at all. One wonders: is there some *other* level at which it's taught? Maybe so. But I'm not talking about either remedial or "advanced" comp, each of which has, arguably, more theoretical coherence than the basic required course that is the subject of jokes, moans, complaints, and execrations on the part of everyone I know who has to teach it.[2]

I meet any one of them and we are at a loss to explain how a group of wretchedly educated kids is reborn as a "learning community." They hate to write—I mean, *hate* it—and yet in the current pedagogical regime we are all mandated to split them up into smaller groups so that we "reduce alienation through collaboration." Now miraculously integrated, or at least integratable, everybody sits around, largely talking of who said or did what to whom last night in the dorm, while the teacher either discreetly stands back or confidently strides about urging still deeper levels of collaboration. All of this takes place in the all-too-human embrace of the "process model." An especially nice thing about this model is that whatever scriptable scrap eventually struggles to the decisive moment of some final draft is deemed to be the product of a "recomposer" who has "entered into a transaction with the text." This means he or she can pass the course.

What's going on here? I got interested in composition studies because a former colleague assured me that the field is an exciting, vital one. He's right. *Rhetoric Review*'s regular little section of controversy, "The Burkean Parlor," ought to be a model for many other journals. And for sophistication, one has to look no further than Dana Heller's example from the comparable "Staffroom Interchange" in a recent *College Composition and Communication*, which ponders Derrida on margins as both theoretical provocation and balm for the deeply problematized practice of writing in the margins of student papers. Yet I'm incredulous. Is Derrida a theoretical context for comps, or are comps a (failed) theoretical context for Derrida? Nobody asks.

Composition themes comprise the most massively *mindless* writing I've ever read—and read, and read. (Studies that have to slow down in order to consider a comp or two necessarily falsify the whole experience of reading them, which rather quickly becomes speeded up if one wants to get through a "set." How many sections of comp do the writers of such studies teach? The author of every article in the major professional journals ought to be required to mention how many sections he or she has taught during each semester or quarter for the previous two years.) It does things to you to read pages and pages of such statements as "If I ever come across a person who didn't know who Bart Simpson was, I would question whether they live on this planet" or "Although young children love and care about each other, affection is never used to show these feelings." One thing it does is make you long to read somebody like Derrida—or at least to wish you didn't have to mark so many damn errors in the margins; perhaps, you dream, some theoretical sanction could be found.

The piece by Heller has an interesting scene of instruction: "In the GA office, amid portraits of Virginia Woolf and Talking Heads, we have held forth on what we believe 'works' in the classroom, and our discussions often betray the influence of fashionable, albeit unlikely icons: Lacan, Foucault, Derrida."[3] What would a Derrida do with how carefully deployed the two portraits are? What would anybody do who's ever taught comp about one's own sheer despair at being able to get real intellectual challenge or *substance* into its classroom? In a *Paris Review* interview, William Gass was once asked if he ever taught creative writing. Gass gave the following lofty reply: "I resent spending a lot of time on lousy stuff. If somebody is reading a bad paper in a seminar, it is nevertheless on Plato, and it is Plato we can talk about. Whereas if somebody is writing about their hunting trip—well—where can one go for salvation or relief?"[4] Is it possible to imagine that one day *CCC* will print a piece on how the author has managed, with methodological circumspection, a student "transaction" so wondrous that a collaborative draft about a hunting trip became an alienated meditation on the folly of pure presence in the forest?

During the last semester I taught comp I chanced to read Paul De Man. Or was it Walter Benjamin? I remember that I was near the end of what turned out to be the semester's worst set of themes and I got so enthralled at the following statement that I forgot to mark its source: allegory is a void "that signifies precisely the non-being of what it represents." That night I believe I felt I had a profound insight into themes, so many of which are "allegories," precisely, for things either the students can't represent or that may be unrepresentable. I think the statement may be no less an insight into comp theory. Composition theory, that is, is the sign for hundreds of sections taught by hundreds of instructors reading thousands of essays on what TV commercials mean, or whether women should participate in combat, or my first erection, or what if you were a tree.

   I don't believe I've ever read an accurate description of what it's like to have to teach these sections and read these essays. "There must be something wrong with a fifty-four-year-old man who is looking forward to his thirty-fifth conference of the day," begins Donald Murray, still "fascinated" after some thirty thousand writing conferences (he estimates) since he began the conference method twelve years ago.[5] Such mock-insecurity (unless Murray's whole piece is a parody) is instead what has been offered about comp to fellow professionals for a number of years. I've read few considerations of any sort that appear to have been consecrated in the abysmal drudgery, the depleted time, the sheer futility that comprise the circumstances, I'm convinced, of most of these people. In the first article of a recent issue of *CCC*, there is the following first sentence by Michael Carter: "Every day in our composition classes, we answer the question, what does it mean to be an expert writer and how do writers become experts?"[6] How could most of his audience possibly respond to such a sentence? For myself, the question of *expertise* hasn't come up in any of my composition classes for at least a decade.

   Can it actually be true that no one who teaches comp tries to write about how empty it is as a subject or even how it gets more theoretically empowered as it gets more empty? (Even textbooks seem old-fashioned now; the point is for students to read nothing else but each other's drafts.) Publication about composition has probably never been more lively and searching. Nonetheless, what gets into print is filled with constraint. Atop the rhetorical hierarchy of the value claims that must be kept in place may be the affirmation that we do whatever we do, in our pedagogical heart of hearts, for The Student.[7] My supposition is that no one can revile comp without immediately being accused of reviling students, who are, in turn, a "god term" so professionally ceremonialized that they can only be comprehended from inside the temple; furthermore, anyone who doesn't approach in the right spirit must be sent packing as a person who didn't belong anyway and never believed. Comp teachers include some of the most pious, not to say evangelistic, people I've ever met.

"How on earth was anybody supposed to teach composition?" laments Miles in John L'Heureux's novel, *An Honorable Profession*. "You were dealing with a largely illiterate generation. They didn't read books. They didn't even read newspapers. They had no model for excellence other than television, where even Tom Brokaw said 'between you and I.' And Tom Brokaw was the high point of television literacy. You couldn't count on MacNeil/Lehrer because students regarded MacNeil/Lehrer as a kind of punishment."[8] It seems to me inevitable that such a lamentation would only appear today in a work of fiction because writers are outsiders to teaching. They utter the truth of outsiders—that which should not be uttered—and they utter it shamelessly. "He is a Viking of off-target platitudes," writes Cynthia Ozick about The Student, "and he believes faithfully in household proverbs. He assures himself that he is a member of an *elite* because he has been admitted to a college, but he despises learning and is oafishly contemptuous of it. Wisdom to him is knowledge, knowledge is information, and information—measurable and codifiable and above all certifiable—is a commodity to be bought and sold with the hard currency of grades" (Ozick, 226).

Ozick wrote the best excoriation I've ever read of comp—which to her means therefore comp students—nearly twenty-five years ago. "He is helpless before a societal idea." She continues, "He praises the world exactly as it is. He is a cynic, yet he cannot keep down a single bitter morsel of historical perspective. He is a moral idiot" (Ozick, 226). (Notice that Ozick is writing in "the old days"—as theme idiom has it—before the discovery of gendered subjects, whose grammatical consequences now constitute one of the minor screws in the composition rack.) This is strong stuff—probably stronger today than ever. Ozick, we note, never questions her own pedagogy. She never wonders how much intelligence or sensitivity one can reasonably expect from an eighteen-year-old. She never seems aware that anything follows from how comp is embedded in institutional practices or cultural imperatives. (In fact, she never mentions it was comp that she taught. But how could someone who writes of a freshman that "cultural cliches appeal to him with a vividness that fresh ideas lack" not have taught comp?) She just gets right to The Student before whom all fails. This is, today, the very Student before whom all succeeds. Part of the reason: no excoriations permitted.

Therefore, decades later, in order to study, for example, margins, a contempt for students must be displaced. Heller's strategy is unusually instructive in this regard. He begins his piece by quoting Stanley Cavell on *King Kong*, whose hectic soundtrack evokes the feeling that "the film is more afraid of silence than Fay Wray is of the beast" (Heller, "Silencing," 210). So an argument gets staged whereby we comp instructors, in the interests of a more fruitful "internal struggle" on the part of our students, must be prepared to work at the limits of our own authority and face our own silence. I have already suggested that the fruit of this particular perspective may in fact be one to be picked by the instructor, whose own internal struggle has gotten depleted by far too many comps to read, much less mark.

More interesting, however, is the matter of the beast. What more fugitive, powerful, and illicit sources may have been responsible for this precise figure? I must hope that I will not seem too glib to suggest the author is in fact Fay Wray to his students's Kong. He is a sacrificial victim, horrified before an undifferentiated (or at least combinatory, and therefore monstrous) mass of bestial energy. As with any of us, he can only scream so much, especially when it is incumbent upon the instructor to have to acknowledge that there is fascination to the monster, pity that eventually needs to be given, and a whole host of other, conflicting emotions to be felt, including loathing. But all of this must be displaced. (Or appropriated under the guise of pluralization. Heller's last sentence reads: "And victory over the ape will be won with the sound of many voices, and the strength of one's will to hear the silence" (Heller, "Silencing," 215). It's of course hard to say how much of the anxiety might come, in addition, from reading too much Derrida as well as, or in conjunction with, too many themes.

It's much easier, in any case, to claim that displaced aggression against students is one source of the authority composition theory has. I have not made sufficiently clear how fascinating I think Heller's text is; the contention that marginal comments "turn the page into an arena in which a fight for possession takes place" is typical of how a poststructuralist discourse can revivify even the most commonplace elements in a practice. (But shouldn't the point be that the comp page, like any page, simply *is* a page because a struggle for possession occupies it? Furthermore, isn't the problematic nature of a marginal comment merely a special, or outer, condition of the problematic nature of *any* comment? And, finally, what exactly is a "comment?") In its way Heller's is "a beautiful piece of writing," or "vibrating with eloquence"—which is what Marlowe says in *Heart of Darkness* about the report Kurtz gives to the International Society for the Suppression of Savage Customs.[9] I cite this text to continue the trope of the savage. What abides in the civilizing discourse of both Conrad's colonial text and Heller's representatively theoretical one is a manifest imbalance with respect to the subject of the discourse. On the one hand, this subject is to be acted upon in order to be liberated so that it may come into possession of all Good Things. On the other, this subject—well, recall what Marlowe finds scrawled at the foot of Kurtz's last page: "Exterminate all the brutes!"

As composition studies grow more sophisticated, is one to assume that its own writing is somehow exempt from figurations that cannot undermine its own truisms? Or exempt from conflicted emotions—at the very least—about its own subjects? One can only go on so long about the necessity to "empower" them or "enter into a dialogue" with their "voices." Students don't command much power yet and they pretty much all speak with the same voice. ("Most people are other people. Their thoughts are someone else's opinions . . . their passions a quotation."—Oscar Wilde. A fair enough epitaph to comp, even if I read it in a comp textbook.) So what to do? Marlowe says of Kurtz's peroration that "it gave me the notion of an exotic Immensity ruled by an august Benevolence" (Conrad, 50). No wonder he vibrates. The more "exotic" the field, the more thrilling the benevolence of its rule. "Theorize the Brutes!"

This theory gives me no consolation. I hate comp because at the center of teaching it there is always a moment when I don't want to be benevolent, and I hate the pretense that I have to try to be. Sometimes this moment suggests to me that the whole enterprise is all pretense—professionalized patience, insincere concern, bored judgment, and sheer disgust. The moment isn't ever the result of the sometimes wildly funny crudities of language or phasing (for example, "In the beginning women were socially dead"), which are now the burden of composition instructors throughout the land to theoretically transmute. What enrages me is always a paper either so outlandishly stupid or so thoroughly repellent that I just don't want to deal with it. I'm reminded of a story a former colleague of mine used to tell about a famous critic he knew who did a lot of popularly based writing. When this man retired from teaching, he continued to lecture. Once at a reception afterwards he was asked an especially dumb question. "I don't have to answer that sort of question anymore," the ex-academic replied. This is still another trouble with comp. In no class anyone in the profession of English teaches are there so many instances of *that* sort of question. Indeed, to me comp is virtually *all* that sort. And to teach comp is to have to answer them all. Another thing this colleague used to tell me is that he would write on really awful papers, "I stopped reading here." Now I suppose you can at least call for another draft.

One has the impression that sometimes Ozick, by contrast, never got started reading. Furthermore, there were absurd questions she matter-of-factly dismissed. Of the manifold "illiteracies" of her students, she writes thus: "They are not ordinary man-size illiteracies, a solecism here, a colloquial lapse there. No. As a subliterate my freshman is stunning, he is stupendous, he is beyond mere inspiration: he is, in fact, *sui generis*" (Ozick, 230). What, I wonder, would have been Ozick's response to the following theme, which I would like to quote here entire? I should emphasize, first, that it's not as outlandish as, say, the one a couple of years ago that argued that we are being denied by the media any chance to save ourselves from a battle fleet of a hundred UFOs, which could very well attack the earth in the next month. Second, the theme is by no means as repulsive as the one I got during my last semester on why drunk drivers should be given life imprisonment. I didn't keep copies of either of these anyway.

One I did is a response to an assignment to write about an activity one enjoys in nature. (This is the kind of witless assignment that I seldom eluded completely over the course of a semester.) Rather than predictable versions of pastoral, one student wrote the following:

> What I am about to explain is not an activity I enjoy in nature; It [*sic*] is an action that perplexes me even to this day.
> One summer evening, a few years ago, I was meandering around the trailer court where I lived. The night was quite boring, and I was trying to find something of which to occupy my time. As I unconsciously glanced towards the

ground, I noticed the cutest little frog. Since I am a nature lover, I naturally picked the frog up and began to study it. This amphibious [*sic*] creature held my attention for at least an hour. Then, an idea came to me. Actually, it was a conscious thought. Since the frog was quite soft like kneaded dough, I wondered, "If I throw it hard enough, will it stick to one of the trailers?" Well, of course I had to try this. To my disappointment, I became rather annoyed and continuously repeated the act. I finally gave up when I realized that I was attempted to accomplish [*sic*] what had already proven to me to be impossible.

I know this action seems quite demented [*sic*] to the average person. Actually, I do not know what came over me. All I know is that I was never able to successfully analyze this act, and, truthfully, I do not think I want to know why I did it.

After such knowledge, what pedagogy? Throw the student amid a group of fellows and hope they convince her to change the subject to kittens? Call the thing a "draft," and trust—with my "collaboration," of course—that the student will discover animal rights in herself? Or just play it safe, especially since the writing is adequate enough, and comment on such things as that the first paragraph has only one sentence, whereas the second has far too many? Perhaps it needs more "detail," or a "stronger" conclusion? Certainly anyone who's taught comp for very long can negotiate a safe, efficient passage away from this composition.

I don't remember mine. I believe I was just mute before this theme. Not because of the cruelty; indeed, it takes a certain honesty to risk it, and, perhaps, even more to write the last part of the last sentence. Yet I fear already that I only sound like a comp teacher in responding this way. What would the "interpretive community" the student calls forth, the "average person" so beloved of comp students, think of this theme? My feeling is that such a person would just dismiss it—as demented, loathsome, or whatever; I can imagine an impossibly "average" person saying, in effect, that there is no point in having reasons about things that do not require them, such as why this is a stupid piece of writing. Any sort of person who has ever taught comp, on the other hand, has to have reasons, and of course each one has to have a point.

I didn't want to deal with this paper because it has that note of unabashed breathlessness before some incident in one's experience that older people want to tell younger people to shrug off. I didn't want to deal with it because its peculiar kind of self-absorption passes into cruelty and out again (for example, what happened to the frog?) without having been modified at all. Most of all, I didn't want to deal with it because it's so contentedly, thoroughly false. I read the final assertion as soaked in disingenuousness and finally only a tease—to the student or to me, I'm not sure it matters; the writer wants to know why she did what she did, but doesn't want to confront the fact that she does.

In fact, to the degree that the paper is written to me, what does matter is that I am given the position of restoring the consciousness that the paper has emptied out. Earlier I wrote of allegory. Perhaps this is an additional reason this paper disturbed me so much. How many themes, albeit not with the exquisite falsity of the one I've been considering, only succeed in setting out some action (including an intellectual one) that dangles like a temptation before the fuller, more mature consciousness of the teacher? In this sense, the very subject of composition is divided against itself, student and teacher each impelled to act out separate roles according to the script of experience and its meaning, albeit currently within a pedagogy that "invites" each to substitute for the other while the originary *lack* of some piece of writing can get plugged up with some meaning or significance or purpose during a process of successive drafts.

Maybe not lack. What's *wrong* with themes anyway? Not all of them, for of course some are good or can be made good. But, for me, even the ones that can be made good are too intimate, or complicit, with the ones that can't—the shallow ideas that will never acquire depth, the personal incidents that can never be interesting, or the "unspeakable rites" (to cite Marlowe on Kurtz) that should never be written down at all for another's evaluation. These last especially mark a limit at which, I think, *any* comment is wrong. Not only is this, in turn, yet another thing that's wrong with comp. (In no other course am I virtually forced to enter into a duplicitous relationship with so many students, most of whom don't even know it.) I think of the moment in *Heart of Darkness* when Marlowe meditates in the following manner over the natives—to their credit, they haven't eaten him, and Marlowe is puzzled why—on his ship: "They still belonged to the beginnings of time—had no inherited experience to teach them, as it were—and of course, as long as there was a piece of paper written over in accordance with some farcical law or other made down the river, it didn't enter anybody's head to trouble how they would live" (Conrad, 42). This is one of those moments when Conrad seems to be revealing more than mystifying his own version of the text of colonialism. That is, we authorities intervene into the lives of the unwritten ultimately only to legislate, and our curiosity about their lives is ultimately a function of our impulse to dominate them.

To return to my degraded example: I didn't, and don't, care why the student squashed the frog. For me to respond in any way to the theme would be to try to change in some fundamental sense what it's about. Instead, my feeling remains, let her kill frogs if she wants. It's not my business to teach her about frogs. She'll include them in her experience or she won't. She'll come to need words for froggy dimensions of her experience or she won't. A mere composition classroom is not the place to get all this decided. Too much of what goes on there is not about writing at all, or only about writing because what it's actually about has to be deferred, which students can be forgiven for not wanting to do. My croak of a comp is really about what Ozick would term "the premises of a civilization," and she has a crisp reminder: "For the premises of a civilization, one does not go to the university; one goes to the kindergarten" (Ozick, 233). Come to think of it, it's in kindergarten where students do such things as throw frogs around. There, presumably, teachers can be content to tell them to stop it.

"I have never learned anything except from people younger than myself." —Wilde again. It wouldn't be such a good *mot* if he said what he learned. From freshmen, I'm not sure that I've ever learned much of anything, except my relief at no longer being one. Perhaps I forget an occasional sort of glazed wonderment about how I ever ceased to be one. I don't believe, however, that this wonderment can develop into very much of an insight. In comp, one just keeps bumping up against it, and then staggering away, perhaps burdened once more with the fear that one has *never* made up one's mind about capital punishment or ceased at last to tremble over the possibility that society is based on hypocrisy. Nearly twenty years, and I still don't see how anyone can learn anything teaching comp, except more ways to teach comp. ("It doesn't matter what you do," another, older colleague used to maintain. "It all comes out equally good and equally bad in the end.") On the other hand, I'm now more certain than I've ever been that all of its many, mundane occasions can be of immense theoretical provocation, and this can provide enough motivation—it can even provide a career—to enable just about anyone to plow through another week's set of themes. You just need to be sure to affirm that it's all for the good of your students.

Good luck to these practioneers. Somebody has to do it. As writing becomes yet more dispensable to some sort of postmodernized, electronic cultural literacy, it becomes yet more important for educators to purport not to know this and instead agree with everyone else that writing, of course, should not be dispensable. Certainly those who teach writing ought to be those who want to do it, or at least who can ignore—I should say transform, reconfigure, dialogize—the very conditions I can't.[10] Many must care about their students just as much as they say on every professional occasion that they do. (The comp studies person I know best confides that she's "burned out," and would "do just about anything" rather than face another section. My own department's such person is craftier and rarely faces one.) Nabokov has a reminiscence of his days as a Cornell lecturer in which he refers to "the great fraternity of C-minus, backbone of the nation, steadily scribbling on."[11] My conviction is that those who really do care most care about exactly *these*, because these are the students who stupefy, madden, and challenge most; the average ones don't even provide comedy, as the worst do, much less exhilaration, like the best. Part of my contention, however, is that it is exactly these steady scribblers—who are not so steady anymore and who get B-minus now—who are repressed in composition studies, because they can never be ignored in practice. "In times of the past, sex was something people enjoyed and not thought to be anticipated." It takes either any unusually dedicated teacher or a routinely dedicated theoretician to turn over page after page of such sentences with relish and profit.

What actually happens when theory extends its most un-disdainful, un-Nabokovian embrace to scribblers of such sentences? Much of the rest of my contention is that we'll never fully know, since all the narratives are professionalized on the basis of a theoretical hegemony that assures that the stories are all benign. (Hence, I must trust, the obvious logic of my own quotations.) In his masterful treatment of teaching composition, the estimable Fish (who, we can be fairly sure, doesn't read many themes each week) writes at one point that we cannot "dismiss the narrative of self discovery" that theory often produces, but, he continues, "this is a narrative that belongs properly to a foundationalist hero, to someone who has just discovered a truth above the situational and now returns to implement it."[12] In composition studies, the theory of narrative is immediately convertible into the narrative of theory, which must be either what Fish terms "foundational" each time or at least "situated" only in lieu of foundational truth to come, maybe as early as next semester. Of course in maintaining this I slight how spirited composition journals are, how thoroughly the social nature of learning is emphasized in them, how many teaching strategies are reexamined, and how provocatively disciplinary boundaries are repeatedly opened up. Even if one's own experience simply will not fit into the official narrative, and plods glumly and unregenerately along beneath salvationalist theories, it is no longer possible to deny that the day for composition studies shines ever more brightly. Too bad everywhere the light shines on sections and sections of comp waiting to be taught, each semester, all over again.

I very much agree with Robert Scholes when he states in *Textual Power*: "The real threat to a new secular textuality is not some 'garden variety semiotic practice' that reduces 'realities' to 'small and manageable written documents,' it is a rampant, de Manic hermeticism that supplants realities with the undecidable toils of its own form of textuality."[13] (Scholes is so intent on sneering at Foucault that he almost ignores punctuation. I wouldn't wish, however, that he became more attentive by teaching more comp.) The classroom as a material, pluralized, discourse-ridden, wholly secularized space: this is, for me, the great thing to be learned, and relearned, from comp studies. Therefore, precisely because this space is such a source of its discursive strength, I find its displacement (at best) of how feeble the literal classroom is in which to teach such a great source of despair.

Can it really be that exactly this same classroom is a source of empowerment to others in most unfoundational, happily situational ways? Speaking a while ago to a man I know about how much I hate teaching comp, I was astonished to hear him say he likes it. "They're so fresh, so in need of being taught," he said of his students; I think he meant he wanted to teach them *values*. This is the sort of realization that forces one to acknowledge that, yes indeed, there may really exist in the world "practioneers" who *look forward* to each semester's sections, even all four. (The only man I ever knew who did had soured utterly on teaching literature, so chose to play out his last few preretirement years teaching comp because it demanded nothing from him.) Nonetheless, I can only comprehend them by remembering Kurtz on the natives, or recalling what I read a while ago expressed by the present Michigan State football coach: "I took this job because I love telling kids what to do. I love giving them orders. Threatening 'em. Because they love it, too. Pro head coaches don't get to do that." What to add? Do you have to know exactly what you're doing if you feel so "empowered"? Do graduate professors correspond to pro coaches in the discipline of English? Anyway, to each level of each profession, I suppose, its own consolations, duplicities, and definitions of love.

And to each person's experience of teaching composition her or his own private vision of the unremitting hours bent over drafts or face-to-face with students. I have endeavored to make clear not only my own vision but my grievance because my experience is sweetly consigned to the status of something privatized and "personal" by available public visions of theoretical hegemony. Conrad's Marlowe again: "You can't breathe dead hippo waking, sleeping, and eating and at the same time keep your precarious grip on existence" (Conrad, 42). The compelling thing about comp is that, teaching it, you have to keep breathing it. Its body is so outsized, so unlike anything "garden variety," that what I have been characterizing—and anathematizing—as ugly or dead is indistinguishable from what might have to do with beauty or life.[14] This is of course all the more true if you need this body in order to have something to eat, which could well be the case if your "grip" is either personally or professionally precarious. But this is true not only in such cases. People publish on comp now who've never gotten their feet wet, much less felt threatened.

A Derrida can be admitted by all, but only, as it were, at the margins. (Undecidability must be read out, and students made to stand in for aporias.) Ozick, Conrad, and Nabokov stay out.

Nobody really wants to know what to do with an ugly composition; everybody acts as if cooperation had some value in itself. In sum, the escape into theory is almost complete, a conclusion that may be tested by assessing how many of the moves in professional journals are made with unquestioned confidence that of course every one is flexible, open, pluralized, genderized, empiricized, and so on.

See, for example, an extremely compelling piece by Howard Tinberg, who is identified in a contributor's note as teaching at least two composition courses per semester at a community college. "The low esteem with which classroom instruction is held among theorists and scholars in the field is the most serious problem confronting composition today," he writes.[15] Tinberg tries not to complain about it, and he certainly tries not to complain about his comp load. However, he is amazed that at the 1990 CCCC convention the woman who gave the chair's address admitted to teaching five sections in one semester, and he is far more characteristically sobered when mere "practioneers" are slighted once again at a discussion the next day. In other words, the presence of resentful and hostile emotions in Tinberg suggests at least the possibility of a very different narrative than the official, progressive one, although presumably it is the fact of this narrative that explains his inclusion in the journal, which functions, once again, as a site for theoretical recuperation of messier practical or political facts.

I hope I've made intelligible my wish that I could join the flight. A mere year away from the comp classroom simply isn't long enough to enable me to feel confident. I'm still not sure where I am, and I keep reading about gigantic apes, thinking about dead hippos, and remembering squashed frogs. Sometimes, horrified, I either miss the themes I used to read or, worse, find myself mentally quoting from some of them. I must have read, for example, the following profundum at least a hundred different times: "Everyone is different, and that will never change." But I'd still rather read almost anything else, and, even though we all know that sound pedagogy maintains theme writing should not be oblique, I'd like to conclude by citing Zora Neale Hurston. She avows that her highly personalized ethnographic effort, *Mules and Men*, was, as with all she wrote, "like the piece of string out of a ham. It's not the ham at all, but it's been around ham and got the flavor."[16]

chapter five

DRIFTING THROUGH

THE MLA

A PROFESSION IS, among other things, its conferences, and yet what is any one person actually doing when attending? At the last MLA in D.C., for example, a woman asked me to shout "can't hear!" as a speaker began one of the sessions. I almost asked her to shout herself, and I wanted to ask her if she didn't think she was committing a "gender infraction" in asking me. But I didn't. Should I have? One simply "attends" a conference, as we say. But what sort of behavior is authorized by such attendance? Or is attendance merely an occasion for any sort of behavior, pretty much as it is anywhere else in nonconferenced life? At which session did I hear which speaker on what text that demonstrated the "multiplicity of identity-related acts"?

In the shuttle bus between the Sheraton and the Hilton I overheard a German woman with two interviews, whose husband, she said, is an engineer, ask a Chinese visiting scholar from a Midwest liberal arts college, "Do you think they'll do to Deng Xiaoping what they did to . . ."—but then I missed the name because somebody behind me proclaimed rather loudly that he was "geographically mobile." The German woman seemed to be very nice to the Chinese man, who, in turn, seemed to be trying very hard to give the impression that he was at ease with the energies of the conference. Is geographical mobility a better representation of these energies than ephemeral conversations between a German and a Chinese academic? Or than my notation that such a conversation has something significant to do with the conference?

Small World is the coyly ironic title of David Lodge's romance of transcontinental conferencing, which concludes, inevitably, at the MLA. The text is so well known in the profession that Elaine Showalter urged grad students to read it, during an initial session for them on the conference, in which she cautioned that the executive director, Phyllis Franklin, was not authorized to marry people, recalled how ritualistically the comical titles of certain sessions are always mentioned in the piece on the conference that always appears in the local newspaper, and advised no talk about anything except politics and the weather in the elevators. Showalter wasn't worried about the best representation of the conference, but she did reveal a witty consciousness about how it abides as a fondly represented, not to say ceremonialized, thing.[1] She gave no clue to her hearers, however, about what any one of them might do with such a consciousness.

Lodge writes that the "megaconference" that is the MLA is "no kind of fun" for candidates who want jobs or chairmen who have to interview them, "but for the rest of the members it's a ball, especially if you like listening to lectures and panel discussions on every conceivable subject."[2] But is it a ball, even if you like to listen to what's spoken outside as well as inside the conference rooms? And what about those who get to speak? I especially recall another conference this past year when I beheld at last one of the hottest names in the profession. He glowed to his audience as he confidently rocked on his heels and tossed jaunty asides away. We glowed back at him and chuckled.

Certainly none of Lodge's principal characters attends the MLA for anything so frivolous as mere "fun." Where they are not desperate for love they are desperate for recognition—subjects that such an impeccably sophisticated occasion as the MLA has installed into official discourse (if only as, respectively, "sexism" and "politics") but has not institutionalized. (Can one now imagine a session, "Sex During the MLA?") It may be one of the curiosities of any conference that it aims potentially to institutionalize the total of the experience that can be brought to it. Meanwhile, one could ask, what to do among the unincorporated or failed fragments—the trivial incidents that nonetheless have some implication in what a paper will refer to as the "torsional relation of the discourses," or the stray vacancies that have not yet been recuperated as the "instrumentality of the particular moment of its composition"? I don't believe that there is a master narrative of the MLA. There is an official one, distributed among the official sessions. What I want to propose here is the unofficial one of drifting, in Roland Barthes's sense of the word, or traveling, in a somewhat more general economy.

At D.C. I met a friend who was only interested in the one session on the one canonical writer who constitutes his field. That's all. He doesn't drift. How many, I wondered, among D.C.'s eleven thousand were so exclusively authenticated—if not with one interest, then with one luncheon date to keep, one luminary to see at last, or, perhaps best of all, one paper to read? How to tell? How to tell the narrative of the great many more, as once again it seemed to me, who sit edgily in chairs before sessions begin, congregate nervously in halls or lobbies, instinctively check the badge of anyone near whether talking to them or not, and veritably groan with the need for contact of some kind—any kind? This time I recalled at one point the 1984 D.C. convention, where the most sheerly exuberant people I noticed (all the cash bars having resembled, as usual, hastily concocted department meetings where nobody knows the chair) were some watching the Redskins playoff game in the Sheraton lobby. I had expired there in despair myself, having realized too late that I had misread the program, wherein the single session I had most wanted to attend was clearly given as taking place in the Hilton.

The sheer size and variety of today's MLA present immense experiential problems to any single individual. Drifting is a solution. What if you don't? At one point I mused upon what might be included in someone's list of an ideal MLA: delivering a well-received paper, meeting an old friend from grad school, hearing another paper that decisively confirmed the direction of one's own work, having lunch with an eminent critic who allowed that one's own paper obliquely confirmed the direction of his or her own work, ignoring the convention completely for both an afternoon and an evening, buying all the most desirable books at the best publisher's booth for a full 50 percent discount, and having sex (preferably not encompassing both afternoon and evening) with an assistant professor from a university one had never heard of who admitted afterwards being "terribly impressed" with one's own paper.

How many are there, however, for whom such a story would not so much be too cynical as just too overdetermined? It may well be that the majority of conventioneers aspire to nothing so grand, so saturated in all the imperatives of the profession itself so formally convened. "There is not a single moment of life from which one cannot extract forces, provided one knows how to differentiate it and combine it with others," states Foucault.[3] What's the trick? What's the trick, especially if you've read Foucault, who elsewhere provides a fair enough description of the MLA as both disciplinary formation and experiential fact: "Power has its principle not so much in a person as in a certain concerted distribution of bodies, surfaces, lights, gazes; in any arrangement whose internal mechanisms produce the relation in which individuals are caught up" (Foucault, *Discipline*, 202). Just so; one attends any convention to be caught up, it would seem.

My own feeling, however, is that one attends simultaneously to extricate oneself, or perhaps rather to see if and how one can do so. That is, amid the disciplinary classifications, systematic distribution of themes, institutional affiliations, regulated times, official sites, ritualized exchanges, and highly saturated contexts, there is ceaselessly available the moment wherein one either enacts one's own subjective negotiation with something that is not MLA or else one does not do so because there is nothing that is not MLA. People attend the MLA for many reasons, even if the MLA values only one or two of them. One reason some attend is to travel through all the reasons, or anyway get caught up in as many as possible and see how they feel.

At any MLA it is possible to have another impossible fantasy: not only to be able to attend *every* session but to be able to hear every convention-saturated word. Since one can't, what consolation? I believe there is only one: drifting. In *The Pleasure of the Text*, Barthes makes drifting equivalent to the atopic, the asocial, as well as to the intractable, the stupid, and even the suicidal.[4] Drifting is not based upon a principle of denial; idealizing is. (Hence the despair of ideals either unrealized or unrealizable.) Drifting, furthermore, is based upon logical contradiction; idealizing abhors such contradiction. (Part of the "monstrosity" of D.C. is the fact that it immediately defeats even the fantasized logic of total attendance—which may be why there are now so many more smaller conventions, where it is still possible to imagine oneself running in and out of all the rooms scheduled for every time period.) "It is the very rhythm of what is read and what is not read that creates the pleasure of the great narratives," writes Barthes. "Has anyone ever read Proust, Balzac, *War and Peace*, word for word?" (Barthes, *Pleasure*, 11). At the MLA one can indeed meet people who have read all the great narratives word for word—or at least listen to papers given by ones who present themselves as such people. Over against each one I would set Barthes's scandalous antihero of a reader "at the moment he takes his pleasure," which partakes equally of what is not, as well as what is, the totality of the officially given.

But such a scandal seems to me to be very difficult to enact, much less conceptualize. Drifting lies in the rhythm of what is attended and what is not attended. What might be most difficult is avoiding making such attendance into a project. Furthermore, the pleasure of drifting ideally exists at all times as available. But again, what is not programmed? I remember a fatigued moment in the Sheraton lobby when I happened upon a sheet announcing a special issue of a magazine devoted to a consideration of pleasure "in all its forms." Had I only found myself drifting into another version of attendance?

One can, I suppose, ignore how utterly enmeshed one is at today's MLA, and how fatefully subject to discipline. I've mentioned my friend of the one session. People also come to an MLA to read their papers, then leave. Have they in fact attended the convention at all (its variously representative aims as well as the social participation upon which such aims are predicated) or reinstituted attendance, only in its negative form? What about those who drop in to one or two sessions, then retire to the homes of hospitable friends, or local museums, or hours-long drinks in the lobby with years-unseen colleagues? An MLA remains, after all, an Event but also an event that provides a pretext for any number of any one person's quite other events—and yet drifting away is not the same thing as drifting, especially if one enters the waters in order not to get wet. I've also known the father of a man who came along for an evening of women's caucus entertainment in order (he hoped) to see lesbians dancing, a student who attended an afternoon in New York solely to see what William Empson looked like, and a now-retired former colleague who told me that the best time he ever had at an MLA was one afternoon at a Palmer

House bar drinking with a prostitute who insisted she could tell a convention of English professors from a convention of lawyers. "One of the primary objects of discipline is to fix," remarks Foucault in an aside. "It is an anti-nomadic technique" (Foucault, *Discipline*, 218). But how can a discipline *prevent* nomads, especially if it is not so easy to fix the boundary separating wandering away from wandering through?[5]

What should an impeccably affixed MLA member be interested in? Only certain things? Just one thing? Everything? Gilbert Murray was once asked if he was interested in incest. "Only in a very general sort of way," the Regius Professor of Greek replied.[6] In the first time slot of the late D.C. convention just past was a session entitled, "The Muse of Masturbation." If one isn't interested in such a session, how is one supposed to respond to it? With outrage? A bemused smile? One could argue that either response is a legitimate, if minor, pleasure of attending the convention—and, furthermore, that drifting into and then out of *some* sort of response (as opposed to the room of the session) is more or less the most compelling theoretical desideratum these days, when only a very general sort of interest in just about anything has replaced some clear basis for excluding at least a few things.

Of course subjects or authors are excluded. The interest that does obtain proceeds, as always, along the lines of scholarly specialization rather than impressionistic whim. Legitimating subjects continues to be what the MLA convention is, in part, all about. Yet when what is programmed is incessantly lambasting the familiar, comfortable, and canonized as a function of celebrating the marginal, unrecognized, and globally diverse, it is in a sense easier than ever before to drift. Similarly, now that all is discourse, what of it that is spoken inside the meeting rooms abides now as far less securely demarcated from what is spoken either before or after the session begins. Between sessions I chanced to hear one man who seemed to be speaking about his paper declare, "Sex in Chaucer is . . ." I deliberately declined to hear the completion. I'm not sure why. It may have struck me for a moment as more enjoyable to imagine myself how the statement could be completed. Maybe I had some instinctive sense that any completion would just be a displacement of a more fundamental presence. Of course in any case it is the displacement that is interesting, not the presence, there being no such undeconstructable thing. It's very easy, as I say, to drift.

Yet such an example illustrates just as much the problem of drifting because it is too officially enabled. Let me offer another instance. Late one afternoon I happened to pass a woman who was saying to another, "I'm not sure if I want to go to the Romantics' cash bar." I smiled at the image of Wordsworth welcoming guests while Dorothy poured the wine. But was the woman's perfectly sensible hesitation an example of what inside the meeting rooms would be termed a "legitimating function" of the convention itself? Could my smile have been a "decontextualizing move," even a registration or "mark" of "spectatorial consciousness"? How to avoid feeling arch about one's responses? When the more commonplace discourse outside the meeting rooms relaxes from the rigors of that inside them, one only attends an MLA now, I believe, to discover that the outside is in fact unlocatable. The theoretical mandate for "reinscription" or "recuperation" is everywhere. One year I spoke briefly to a man who appeared to feel that the convention had been ruined for him because the subject of the president's address had not been published beforehand. What to reply? That such a fact could have freed him to circulate more carelessly, or that the president may have lately been reading deconstructionist critiques against writing-in-the-name-of-the-father? Years ago I met another man whose sole reason for attending was to jockey for position at as many publisher's booths as he could in order to gain maximum advantage for the 50 percent buy-off on the last day. Again, what to conclude? Fetishizing texts is another thing the MLA is all about, although lately a rather retrograde notion, because there is plenty of sheer textuality (incipient or otherwise) elsewhere about to consume.

At D.C. there could be observed the fullest display of how great is the disciplinary investment in looking for gaps, nodes, and interstices for the interpretation of textual practice. The once almost terroristically theoretical terminology such as "valorize" or "erasure" has been completely domesticated, and the psychologistic vocabulary of "displacement" or "scene" is thoroughly in place in order to elucidate "embedded narratives" or "gender inflected interpretive strategies." No greater professional triumph can be secured at the MLA than to fix the moment when a text becomes "unsettled" or "undone." (In one session a speaker veritably *pounced* upon the "subversive rupture" of the logic she had been tracing in the "conflicting agendas" of her author. This represented a very different sort of zeal from that rising off the pedestrian thematics of another session's paper, whose author failed to restrain a knowing smile as he roundly declared "the fearful truth in one's psychic imagination.")

But what sort of migratory triumph—or just installation— can be made? Is it just to enjoy the lush, self-enclosed dance of critical idiom for its own sweet sake? (That is, quite apart from its hermeneutic or discursive labor in any specific instance.) At the last MLA in L.A., I heard a word that I've never heard or read since: "deontified." It was recently in D.C. that I had a brief discussion over whether it is currently more fashionable to say "rupture" rather than "gap" in one's discourse. Is a theoretical moment that has so much invested in looking for either one more or less vulnerable to what it can't recuperate or is unable to (re)inscribe? One thing for certain: this moment uses up so many apparently simpler or naive perspectives that the canniness of drifting consists of willingness to appear dumb, or just plain stupid, before an "ultrafied logic" whose consequence, as somebody joked, is that "you can't write to your mother without putting brackets around the 'm.'"

Does a system elicit an ultimately comic perspective from one who inhabits it by drifting? I believe this is too programmatic. Just as no convention is in a constant relationship to its program, no conferee is in a constant relation to the convention. The program, indeed, might be compared to a travel itinerary structured to bring the tourist to the Great Sites (to which might be compared the Great Subjects or the Great Critics), and yet permitting enough diversion or free time along the way so that one might engage in vulgar commerce or somehow mingle with the natives. (But who would be the natives at an MLA? The hotel workers? At another convention this past year I had a pleasant conversation with the man who wheeled away the movie projector from a session—and soon revealed himself to be a professor in charge of media conventionwide.) The experienced tourist knows that often the marginal experiences prove more memorable than the official ones, which can be so crowded, familiar, or just inert that one may as well have stayed home.

"Sightseeing is a kind of collective striving for a transcendence of the modern totality," writes Dean MacCannell in *The Tourist*, "a way of attempting to overcome the discontinuity of modernity, of incorporating its fragments into unified experience."[7] This is not a bad definition of conventioneering, even if the most decisive difference is that the convention program, unlike the tour itinerary, offers instead an immersion in discontinuity. But a member of the group is not prevented from suddenly finding that the language of the rest is more exotic than the natives. Moreover, someone can just as suddenly grow unsure whether the spectacle of over a hundred people crammed into a hotel room and hushed before the lone voice of a man or woman reading a paper is meant to *be* a spectacle—much less whether one ought to find it moving or absurd.

MacCannell again: "An authentic touristic experience involves not merely connecting a marker to a sight, but a participation in a collective ritual, in connecting one's own marker to a sight already marked by others" (MacCannell, 137). Yet, if something that is not MLA can always be converted into something that is, there will always be, at any MLA, disconnected sights that will never be "marked" by others; the convention is about recognition and its representation, and every convention stages itself within the at-once mobilized and dispersed tension between what is recognized and what is not.[8] Drifting, you not only disconnect yourself but fall into the seduction of a calculation whereby what no one else appears to "mark" becomes the only thing worth seeing. MLA members are of course impeccable in their discretion. No one purported to notice a woman nursing her baby in the front row of one session, and no one gaped one evening at the Famous Critic eating scrambled eggs and pancakes (in the company of two women who each looked as if she wanted to eat him). On one panel: a real Harvard professor in a real bow tie. Was he or anyone else amused at the lineaments of caricature? At another session: one female panelist in a bright lavender jacket along a solid row of grey male tweed. How many in the audience wondered about sexual politics, the semiotics of professional fashion, or something else more gratuitous? The stray moments when one's soberest attention *fails*, the hopelessly fugitive moments when one is *elsewhere*—such moments are private, plural, uncomprehensive, perhaps uncomprehending and certainly unrepresentable. It is no different with the surface of words; the most fashionable D.C. discourse was so complicit with one's own subversive desires for "mere" enjoyment that it can be all too inescapable to feel physically *present* when a speaker is saying "absence challenges the certainty of written knowledge," or questioning whether a text is capable of "sincere, or even authentic textual self-recovery."

At an earlier MLA I once happened to be sitting among a group of men when one rose up and radiantly moved away to the sudden call (for so it had been mysteriously given unto him) of the rarest of boons: an *on-the-spot* interview. (It had been about an hour since he had delivered his paper.) Exactly where was he ascending? I recalled the cavernous interviewing room. How could such a thing really be possible? I felt I was witness to a professional miracle. Yet recognition, of course, spreads. At the MLA one feels it as if it were a species of living stuff, to be produced, consumed, and reproduced. Some gets represented, used up, represented again, and some does not. According to what basis? Jacques Derrida has an essay for a conference (which is therefore, to him, in part on conferences) in which he finds "the dominant generality of representation" to be "authority." What authority exactly dictates what representation is less Derrida's concern than the very category of representation itself, which acts, at least since Descartes or Hegel, "to determine the apprehension of whatever it is that is of concern or interest in any relation at all."[9]

And at the MLA? Is there finally anything more to say than that there remains (like a kind of residue) much of no concern or interest because there is so *much* of concern and interest—all of it re-presentable? But what of that which is not? Like my own bemused wonderment at the on-the-spot interview, is what eludes, meanders by, or deviates from authoritative representation necessarily fated to be, as we say, "unrepresentative"? Or does it have its own errant life after all in the representational machine, which produces, as in the case of the miraculously chosen interviewee (I don't know if he got the job), a represented subject who is equally a representing subject? The questionableness of drifting arises from the fact that it fails consistently to perform the work of representing itself, like a traveler subject to forgetting where he's going or where he's been.

How would drifting presume to represent itself? Ultimately, I believe, by means of anecdotes. In *Teletheory*, Greg Ulmer several times discusses the function of anecdotes as one form of "speculative" organization, although his primary interest is in those "embedded in the abyss of a theoretical discourse."[10] What I want to claim myself is that anecdotes enunciate a knowledge more miniature, diverse, random, and incidental than theory, whose narrative is sponsored by some governing idea. The idea of an anecdote, in contrast, is far less explicable, without the conclusive unity between story and explanation. Do anecdotes, furthermore, propose a self whose identity is akin to the ideally multiplied one of the traveler? It would seem to be so. In traveling, that is, things "just happen" to us, our experience can be consistently accidental, and if we want to add it all up we may not be entirely free of the feeling that it may not add up to anything at all. There are many stories that can be told—not only, as we say, the "representative" ones.

So I'd like to conclude my account of drifting through the MLA with two anecdotes, one about boundaries kept, the other about boundaries crossed. At least I think the anecdotes are about boundaries. I'm more certain they're about selfhood—specifically, the kind that conferences at once represent and fail to represent. Drift as you please at the MLA, it's very difficult not to coalesce as yourself, much as you trust you can either exceed or elude who you are, in the interests of finer or shallower energies.

Next to me when I boarded the plane to fly out to the 1983 L.A. convention was a severe, owlish chap. Surely *not* an English professor, I thought. But sure enough, soon he pulled out a copy of *Pride and Prejudice*, produced a pen, and peered at the first page. "Excuse me," I emboldened myself, "are you an English teacher?" He allowed as how he was. "Going to the MLA?" Curt assent.

Such was the full extent of our intercourse. I already had a copy of the *New York Times Book Review* in my hands, and eventually, somewhere during the time we bumped over the Rockies, I produced my own novel. By then my fellow conferee was well into what was obviously his convention paper, carefully laid out on top of his leather bookcase. He never looked up until we landed and the plane came to a full stop. I reflected that I could have been sitting across from the Rev. Mr. Collins, and I thought of the sweatshirt that declares that its wearer "would rather be reading Jane Austen"—a motto to which would have to be added in his case, "for strictly professional reasons."

And yet he was a version of me for all that, and may have taken me to be a version of him. My destinational query may have been too sprightly, already, to him, a version nonattendance, just as his reply struck me as far too dry, already a definitive confirmation of attendance. Enjoyment? Quite possibly a grimmer term for him than me, though not without its irony, inseparable from mine. No matter what his behavior may have indicated, had I been able to discuss with him what he took to be the significance of attending the MLA, I want to doubt that his answer would have been fundamentally different from mine. In the words of Walter Stone (in an older idiom than I've been citing, since it was published over thirty years ago):

> A man's profession is not a mere appendage to life and ought not to be. It ought to be just as full of meaning and have just as much connection with eternity as any of his other activities. The Convention is the ritual of his profession; it puts his other activities in perspective with the activities of his colleagues, and his past in perspective with his present. It teaches him where he stands in the world of his peers and where he stands in the history of himself. For in that permanent world outside time and place he meets precisely himself.[11]

I could put our agreement this way: although the convention toward which we headed was nothing if not saturated in more disciplinary relations than either of us would ever directly experience, it remained a site in which we could confront our own identities nonetheless. And who did we find? Ourselves—consuming because others were producing, or delegated while others went in their own name. It is impossible at the MLA not to meet oneself or not to repeat the structure whereby someone else reappears as oneself.

Is it possible *not* to go in your own name? A concluding story.

My own main purpose in flying to L.A. was not to attend the MLA. That year I was not even a member. So when I decided to attend I had no badge. A badgeless MLA being inconceivable (since much of the representational foundation would then collapse, and even drifting would become impossible since there would be no structure from which such an activity could veer), I had to get a badge in order to fit. One day I secured a badge for a single session. Another day a friend loaned me a badge for another session. After that session I chanced to find still another badge on a hotel corridor floor. With this last badge I felt I had an identity at last, or rather I had a "floating signifier" that could enable the matter of my identity to be dispensed with. And so it went. No one ever took me for the man whose name was on the badge.

In D.C. three years later I met a colleague from my own university. He introduced me to the man with whom he had been chatting. This man looked at my badge, I looked at his. On his read the very name of the badge I had found in L.A.—and so shaking hands with him felt rather too uncomfortably like literally meeting myself. Is it not a perfectly logical inversion of the structure whereby someone else reappears as oneself that oneself may reappear as someone else?

Badges of course enable recognition to be conducted according to professional or institutional hierarchies. Badges require subjectivities to be represented officially. My meeting this man (at once not-me and me) could only have been possible through the signifying system of badges, and yet the significance of the meeting could neither be quite recognized or represented by the system. I wasn't sure if I had drifted into the system or out of it. Had I exceeded the convention framework or vanished beneath it?

Years later, again in D.C., I was especially struck by a statement from one session about "the life of signs at the heart of social life." I recalled my above meeting five years ago. Again it seemed to me to have no professional use, and I believe I relaxed into the memory more confidentially, without very much resistance. I hadn't been enjoying this past year's MLA very much anyway. Its edges felt too rounded, the days had been too strenuous, I had felt too completely myself. The moment of the earlier D.C. meeting didn't make me feel fulfilled, just perhaps better dispersed, for drifting through the MLA is drifting in and out of signification, and it remains possible to enjoy some crossings for what they get rid of as well as for what they affirm.

chapter six

BEING A WHITE MALE

THE CONTEMPORARY academic white male need look no further to understand his plight than a moment in the first chapter of Marianne Hirsch's new *The Mother/Daughter Plot: Narrative, Psychoanalysis, Feminism*. Hirsch, "inspired" by what has been termed a "poetics of location" within "the rapidly expanding field of psychoanalytic feminist theory," wants to say who she is. So she has been writing, she states, "as a woman, a teacher, a daughter, a mother, a feminist (should I add a heterosexual, a Jew, an immigrant, middle class, an only child, a mother of sons?) within the institutions of patriarchy, of motherhood, of literary studies, of feminist studies, of the university in the United States (should I add of marriage, of divorce, of the Ivy League, of Comparative Literature and French Studies, of the development of Women's Studies?)."[1] Who is she then? It appears that she locates herself not only to disclose that she has no secure location. She writes herself only to falter over the necessity for a stable identity. There are too many categories available to her. The very space of location is in fact a decentered one. The first thing to say about being a white male is, on the other hand, that its site is eminently secure, its identity indisputably stable—in part because what a white female is has become so luxuriantly problematized and vexed.

It may be the last thing to say. Most academic men I know—their consciousness raised by feminism, not to say weighed down—don't say anything much, even among themselves. Everybody knows what a white male is, and nobody wants to be one. I know a man with a recent Ph.D. who learned that he lost a tenure-track position because the department had to hire a woman in order to adhere to administration-enforced affirmative-action guidelines. He's a white male. What should his attitude be? He just told me the news flatly. I wasn't sure if he really had no bitterness or was trying hard to have none. The same evacuated tone was apparent on the part of the chairman of a department at a major university when he mentioned to me a while ago, in a letter, that his administration has sent down the word that no white males are to be hired by his department for at least the next two years. A former student of mine, now a graduate student, was more sarcastic when he detailed a class last year in which one of the country's most prominent feminists ridiculed the way he both stood and spoke while giving a report as being typical of a "straight white male." "What could I say?" my friend asked, and then tried to joke that he could have promised his teacher that he'd set to work on becoming gay.

Even a year later, this is now a more difficult joke to make. Gay studies have become cutting-edge at conferences and fashionable on the job market. Homophobia has become as officially abhorrent as misogyny, and far more quickly. I want to say more about the relationship between gay studies and feminism in a moment. Here at the outset I will emphasize merely that gays have become academically ascendent in very much the same way as feminists. Consider Ed Cohen at the end of the first paragraph of a recent essay: "During the last twelve months, I have turned thirty; moved from San Francisco to New York City; completed a highly enjoyable first year as a tenure-track assistant professor. . . . Furthermore, all this occurred in the shadow of the most emotionally demanding part of my life, where in therapy, body work, meditation, yoga, and especially among friends and colleagues, I am attempting to imagine and create for myself an urban male sexuality that affirms the desirability of my 'gayness' in late twentieth-century, postmodern, 'postfeminist,' post-Reagan, post-AIDS America. But let's not talk only about me."[2] Cohen cavorts among categories more excitedly than Hirsch. The point I would make is merely that, once again, it would be scarcely conceivable for a white male to begin a text in this manner. A white male is still understood to be, in addition, heterosexual. This lamentable, because privileged, heterosexuality functions as yet another reason for the white male to keep his place. Most do, and not only because they enjoy positions of power already.

It may be objected that my examples are purely anecdotal and impressionistic. So they are. I've already discussed in my preface the feminist co-option of "the personal" in the writing of discursive prose. One result has been a second thing that can be asserted about being a white male: its knowledge claims in the academy have been reduced to the status of the transparent, hearsay, ephemeral, personal, or "subjective," all the better so that the category can abide as abstract, familiar, and, above all, essentialized. This last is the crucial installation. In an interesting rejoinder to some criticism of his original contribution to the collection of essays, *Men in Feminism*, Andrew Ross notes: "Perhaps . . . this critique of essentialism is 'rather tired' or 'by now rather familiar' for feminist theorists, but this does not make it any less cogent for a larger world . . . in which the initiation of men and women into sexual politics is still so hegemonically informed by this mutually exclusive division between anatomical groups."[3] Neither men nor women, that is, are finally, or essentially, what their respective bodies (including emotions and intellectual capacities) dispose them to be. Men, no less than women, become what they are in terms of specific cultures; neither is simply born as the gender that each eventually comes to be because of social articulation. Thus runs the truism. In practice, however, such academic intelligence is not equally sustained. Even in the impeccably—not to say painfully or even comically—theorized pages of *Men in Feminism*, the sheer heterogeneity of what a woman is gets developed beside the presumed homogeneity of what a man is. Of course most of the contributors would not want to maintain that some irreducible commonness of both experience and construction is actually true for all men. Nonetheless, the assumption persists, and the point about it, I think, is not only to insure that maleness remains the "hegemonic" category. Maleness is simply not *interesting*. It is already well enough known, if not too well known.

Of course this is changing. *Men in Feminism* can be quite strikingly contrasted with a more recent collection of essays, *Engendering Men*, subtitled "*The Question of Male Feminist Criticism*," one of whose editors writes in the opening essay that, among other things, men ought to "make their own oppressive structures (ideological, social, psychological) *present* for critique, rather than hiding them under a veil of abstract musing."[4] One reads elsewhere of emergent programs in masculinist studies, clearly empowered by the feminist project and the interdisciplinary interrogation of gender. Maleness is gradually becoming problematic, multiple, historically variable—interesting. But such interest as it can be made to possess as a field for academic "inquiry" will proceed, as many of the essays in *Engendering Men* make clear, very slowly. Far more important, male criticism must acknowledge (as the opening essay by the coeditor does) that it is feminism which inaugurates the male project. Furthermore, the project only proceeds by deploying itself very warily in terms of a sophisticated theoretical method that will always retain more value, power, and political urgency. Of course the coeditor, Joseph Boone, doesn't say this explicitly. There is much to say about any sort of academic interest in men, and especially by men, which still can't be said because it isn't politically correct to do so.

Up to a point, what man would want to dispute anymore that enough is already comprehended on the basis of male experience? What teacher of literature, for example, has not grown weary of still another story in which it is inevitably a young male who undergoes the hard passage from innocence to experience, or of yet another poem in which a vigorous male voice is played out against the silence of a female? Some time ago I gave a paper at a conference in a session on travel writing. Hemingway's *Death in the Afternoon* was central to my argument. The most theoretical of my fellow panelists bristled at the very name. "Hemingway!" he cried. "What about Gertrude Stein? Do you realize this whole session hasn't mentioned women at all?" I hung my head in shame for a moment. So hung the collective head of the audience—mostly male, all white. Of course the session had had nothing to do with gender. This wasn't the point. It *should have*. We might have thought we knew better. Instead we failed once again at least to realize that our discourse had been another variant upon the universalizing one of patriarchy, which presumes, among other things, that its own constituent elements provide the means whereby any subject can be treated and disposed.

Understood this way, it is hardly any wonder that feminist theory—whether spoken by men or women—is disinclined to be interested in maleness. Patriarchy has had the consequence that virtually any interest in anything is ultimately an interest governed by male orthodoxies and phallic positions. The critique of patriarchy, therefore, has disdained the one thing that patriarchy took for granted: the exemplary fact of male experience. Indeed, in one quite forceful sense feminism constitutes a reasoned rebuke to men for their sheer presumption in taking all experience exclusively to themselves. It is not merely that male experience effaces or subsumes that of women. Stephen Heath writes of "male feminism" in the *Men in Feminism* volume: "His experience is her oppression. . . . feminism starts from there. To refuse the confrontation . . . is for a man to refuse feminism, not to listen to what it says to him as a man." (Jardine and Smith, 12). What it says to him as a man is that his very experience is banal, empty, and recuperable only at a larger discursive level that the formulation, "patriarchy," may be said to characterize.

However, what if this experience is homosexual? Does patriarchy endorse it, if it is? *Engendering Men*, as if enacting the repressed of *Men in Feminism*, is absorbed by homosexuality— sufficiently so, it could be argued, that the only way for maleness to hold any theoretical provocation is for it to be investigated as a site for, according to one contributor, "the utopian erotics of modern subjectivity," which is far more openly and cleanly expressed by homosexuality than heterosexuality (Bone and Cadden, p. 206). It's still not entirely clear if, once the heterosexual "mechanism" for "obscuring" the "self-reflexive erotics" of homosexuality is dismantled, males will be less patriarchal; upon this question turns perhaps the most decisive future of male feminist criticism.[5] Meanwhile, there is a third thing about being a white male that remains crucial: one is perforce converted into a patriarch. It is precisely this conversion that Frank Lentricchia contests in a fascinating recent exchange with two of the country's most prominent feminist critics, Sandra Gilbert and Susan Gubar.

"Male is not equivalent to patriarchy," writes Lentricchia about his original article, "That's a one-sentence summary of what in part I was trying to get at."[6] Gilbert and Gubar, on the other hand, would give up the equivalence only very grudgingly, in part because I don't believe they are entirely at ease with what might be gained by women at this moment in history to have to admit any dissonance at all between maleness and patriarchy. What (heterosexual) men gain is all too clear: an intellectual basis for potentially exculpating themselves, man by man, from a discursive consensus (anthropological, psychological, historical, and so on) that feminist theorists have carefully and systematically built up over some decades. Heath writes that men's relation to feminism is an "impossible" one (Jardine and Smith, 1). It becomes quite possible if a common oppressor can be agreed upon.

The two women are responding to the man's original article, which included a criticism of their famous *The Madwoman in the Attic* in the course of arguing for the culturally feminized position experienced by the young Wallace Stevens as he sought to write out precisely how he was embedded within the patriarchal structures of his time. The exquisitely gendered exchange is unusually instructive about how profound are the duplicities that women perceive men to be involved in when they embark upon the suspiciously simple project of trying to represent themselves as men. (The project is somewhat less suspicious—or maybe just less threatening—if the men are gay.) Lentricchia and Gilbert and Gubar can't agree on anything because they can't agree on why what we might term the anguish of maleness (the nuances of its coming-into-existence, the anxieties of its patriarchal placement) is worth representing at all.

"Perhaps Lentricchia not only fears his own dependency on feminist criticism," the women comment at one point, "but also is troubled by the 'autonomy' of critics who don't make a 'fuss' over men. In one of his more hectic moments, after all, he declares that 'the ancient social process called patriarchy' consists also in the oppression of patriarchs. Uneasy lies the head that wears the crown."[7] Just as uneasy, one could comment, lies the head that cannot think without the knowledge that some Other wears the crown, *and is content*. Everybody knows what a white male is, all over again. The sarcasm of Gilbert and Gubar is illustrative of how patriarchy has come to be widely understood as an ideological structure that utterly comprehends male specificity—although, to be fair, the women appear to be mindful of heterosexuals only. Perhaps the most immediately compelling element in the exchange is their reading of the man's "infamous photo" on the back of one of his books as representing a "street-wise tough"—part of a consistent pattern of "virilization-as-defense" by American men of letters who feel themselves threatened by feminization (Gilbert and Gubar, 405). Lentricchia's counter to this reading is fascinating. He writes that his photo fits, if it must, into a Gilbert and Gubar "tradition" that he recharacterizes as one "of self-mocking send-ups of macho stances: not a defense of stereotypical masculinity but its comic subversion" (Lentricchia, 411). In other words, masculinity exists the better to be mocked. However, we want to ask further, can Lentricchia imagine a representation of masculinity without irony? Can any man within feminist discourse? Something of the power of the gay critique is purchased, I think, by its confident affirmative to this question. Lentricchia can only ask, "What, anyway, is *un*stereotypical masculinity in our culture?" But he does not stay for the answer. This interpretive struggle over the photograph dramatizes, I think, that there appears to be no image available of a fully masculine man. (Much of the unarticulated problem turns on some presumption of virility. None of the critics seems willing to speculate whether such an idea is retrograde, progressive, or just absurd.) Is the very thought of such an image instead a scandal? Most likely. Male self-possession is a fraud, based as it must be on a necessary denial or devaluing of so much as the possibility of female self-possession. Everybody knows.

Another thing the whole exchange discloses is that there is at least a fourth feature about being a white male: the identity possesses no representational power. Or at least none of any discursive sort that could be articulated from some cultural space where maleness is *not* convertible into "macho stances" (as it is in movies or professional sports), much less where maleness is at ease with energies that are "self-mocking." (Obviously the equation of homosexuality changes the matter profoundly.) Lentricchia protests that "Gilbert and Gubar take the 'perfect cock' even more seriously than some of us boys do. Certainly more seriously than Stevens does in the poem from which they quote the phrase." Yet his protest is not based on a very confident posture, especially over against that of Gilbert and Gubar, who, throughout, speak from the stance of an aggressive, proud, triumphant feminism. It has triumphed over any contestatory power to represent what a man is.[8] Lentricchia operates as one within a unitary system of categorization, yoked to a totalized system of oppression.

Gilbert and Gubar, quite shrewdly in my opinion, see Lentricchia's reading of Stevens as a writing of his own anxieties about "the feminization of the critical life" (Gilbert and Gubar, 403). Most importantly, they quickly sense, even to perform such a writing is for a man to engage with women in a "competition of victimization" (the women's term, acknowledged from feminist practice) that is outrageous because the very terms of the exchange are those of a feminist theorization, which has rationalized quite away any claim a male might have to gender victimage. What is a man? It is finally not a political moment for a man to say. A man is what a woman says he is—and, in so saying, she frees herself from the traditional, patriarchal saying of her by him. I must trust I've made clear how any male feminist criticism gains both its urgency and its cogency insofar as it participates in this same freeing, which it does by coming out gay.

So what is a man? Ultimately an object for feminist discourse. Insofar as he can't represent himself with his own voice, has anecdotal authority only, and in the most intellectually sophisticated and politically progressive areas of American life must silently endure ideological imperatives, this man is in fact curiously like what a woman is in prefeminist masculinist discourse. In a concluding section of conversation to *Men in Feminism*, its two editors, Alice Jardine and Paul Smith, are discussing the latter's self-conscious, problematized, and possibly sportive use of the word "penetrating" in the opening paragraph of his essay in the volume. Many of the volume's contributors note this usage. All of them appear to wish that it just hadn't been made. Nobody exactly says this, much less that there is an almost audible wish that Smith simply had nothing with which he could effect any sort of "penetration." What Jardine does say at one point is the following: "In a recent public lecture I played with feminism 'penetrating the institution.' Everybody laughed. It's OK for me because I can't penetrate anything" (Jardine and Smith, 255). *Everybody* laughed? All the men? Jardine's blithe dismissal of her little joke could not be in greater contrast to Smith's harried resignation to the abysmal seriousness underlying his own. Ostensibly powerless—or where's the joke?—Jardine speaks with the casualness of one far more subtly empowered. Presumably powerful—or otherwise upon whom would the humor fall?—Smith just doesn't reply. Nowadays, should one wonder if he would if he were gay?

In fact Smith does reply to a sterner reading of his original usage in the following manner: "What would I have been thinking of to write what she says I wrote? I'd have to be a rapist." "Or just a straight white male academic," retorts Jardine. Smith admits it. "But . . ." "But what?" snaps Jardine. "*That's* the problem" (Jardine and Smith, 255). The man and the woman are repeating in shorter, simpler, and cruder form the gender scenario of Lentricchia versus Gilbert and Gubar (as well as, I believe, that proposed by the *Engendering Men* contributors). The same reductive conversions are made from the female position, and with the same principled operation. From the male position there once again issues an admission—and then there is essentially nothing else to say. A (straight) white male (academic) has written. In Smith's case he's done so with an explicit phallic foregrounding. He shouldn't have, in part because he needn't have. It would have been scarcely less crude to have made an analogy to a football game. Everybody already knows about such things. Therefore he must not say so.

I don't believe that saying so necessarily suggests an emergent alignment of the suffering male today with that of the suffering female up until yesterday. Saying so, however, does disrupt the careful, even fragile, symmetry upon which contemporary feminism is based. Women today can make jokes about penetration because men can't. Heath explains this unequal equality very incisively and is worth quoting at some length: "What is difficult for men aware of feminism is not to imagine equality for women but to realize the inequality of their own position: the first is abstract and does not take me out of my position (naturally women should be equal with me); the second is concrete and comes down to the fact that my equality is the masking term for their oppression (women are not equal with me and the struggle is not for *that* equality)" (Jardine and Smith, 25). Precisely. Therefore to trace how this logic may be reconcretized in order to demonstrate how women's inequality functions in the academy today as a masking term for their superiority to men can only be done under the suspicion (at the very least) that phallic orthodoxy is merely being confirmed once more. In what interests is one going to claim that the criteria upon which jobs are advertised ("Women and minorities encouraged to apply") institutionalize sexism against men at the present time? In what demonstrable ways is one going to maintain that the enormous professional opportunities made possible as a result of feminism—conferences organized, topics for articles and books solicited—enhance this same institutional bias? In today's unequally equal times it can hardly be self-evidently stated, but it can be stated: gender *pays off.*

Gay studies demonstrate this all over again, as well as masculinist ones inseparable from a gay agenda. That is, as long as feminism sets the terms for any agenda; part of Gilbert's and Gubar's dismay at Lentricchia is at the prospect of another agenda whose formations (patriarchy as divided against itself) would invariably, they maintain, shatter their own. Gender pays off as long as what the male gender is stays grounded. It has been common in the academy for some years now to hear a voice at meetings that speaks up by commencing, "As a woman, I . . ." I've never heard anyone object, just as I've never heard another voice beginning, "As a man, I . . ." (It's probably just accident that I haven't yet heard still another voice uttering, "As a gay man, I . . .") One of the women in *Men in Feminism* chides that "women, in the name of women, cannot perform the same universalizing operation as men" and therefore concludes: "the male—or at least the white Western male—as things stand now, cannot be excessive and cannot occupy the margins" (Jardine and Smith, 73). The consequence is that women have come to occupy what might be termed the "universalizing" position (it would come to much the same thing if one wrote "hegemonic" instead), and their paradoxical warrant for doing so is that they occupy the margins.

How inexpressibly more inconceivable it would be to hear still another voice at a meeting announcing itself, "As a white man, I . . ." It will have been objected that I have been neglecting the adjective—while investigating another, more fashionable one—for the noun. Gender, after all, is one thing, race another. In fact, within the discursive framework of feminism, this aims not to be the case. Gender and race are continually proposed as the same thing, and the best certification of this equivalence is the very category: white male. There are, on the other hand, no white females. Hirsch, for example, whose happy multiplication of herself I began by quoting, does not "locate" herself by race. Is a reader to take her whiteness for granted? Perhaps. Certainly the problem with there being white females arises only when the adjective has to be employed—usually by black females whose consistent complaint has been that white females have taken their own racial category for granted, and hence made what a woman is a much too homogeneous, exclusive, and bourgeois entity. ("Those early theorists and practioneers of feminist literary criticism were largely white females who, wittingly or not, perpetrated against the Black woman writer the same exclusive practices they so vehemently decried in white male scholars," charges Deborah McDowell, for example.)[9] It is the burden of white maleness to address the rupture that invariably opens in feminist discourse as a result of this charge. Feminists of both races summon the category into being, thereby exteriorizing the disruptive adjective from within feminist practice and displacing it onto men. Lentricchia makes the following accusation against Gilbert and Gubar: "Feminism of the sort they profess is another form of it: gender unmodified by differences of class and race" (Lentricchia, 412). I wish he had noticed how his very own category of a white male functions to provide at least some modification. Men merit the racial register because women don't—and women don't because men do. White females appear circumspect and socially nuanced over against white males. Therefore, while the essential difference of gender can be promoted, the possibly greater determinations of race get deployed in order to deepen the totality of male oppression.

The conceptual moves in all this are exactly those studied by Barbara Johnson in *The Critical Difference*. In her introduction, she gives what I take to be a now-classic formulation of the ruses of difference: "The differences *between* entities (prose and poetry, man and woman, literature and theory, guilt and innocence) are shown to be based on a repression of differences *within* entities, ways in which an entity differs from itself."[10] Of course there are other ways of examining the consequences of these moves. For example, discussing her suspicion of males who now want to "feminize" themselves, another of the *Men in Feminism* contributors detects sheer envy by men at women's undeniable history of oppression and quotes "a close male friend" who once "sadly" said, "Your position is, after all, ideal" (Jardine and Smith, 238). Just so, a newly empowered enunciative space enriches its ethical advantage by appropriating an even more "ideal" oppression of racism. "Are we stuck once again," the contributor continues, "in a heterosexist perversity thinly disguised as an authoritative intellectual inquiry on 'feminist theory'?" In a sense, "we" are. The more so, however, if we disdain how guilt can migrate, or how victimization can be advantageous. One reason we are stuck is because we continue to expel "them" into every species of absolute otherness—the very thing, one would have thought, that our study of how they employed us would have prevented us from doing—and to whiten our differences among ourselves as differences between them (here more intricately given as "hetero") and us.

Of course the matter is not, finally, very accurately represented, as I have been doing, by employing an idiom of choice or will. Choice and will, we might say, are provocatively irrelevant—as irrelevant as what adherence the smudge of racism has to the actual oppression real men inflict on real women. Or as irrelevant as how an American male has it culturally mandated for him to experience the sheer *whiteness* of his being (which might far more reasonably be expected before the degraded difference of a black rather than a woman). I have been discussing the discursive category of white maleness as utterly separable from its social or material realization. That it cannot be so utterly separated does not, I believe, change the fact whereby the white maleness that "everybody knows" about, and which therefore nobody has to choose to have attitudes about, exists to support a carefully modulated economy of differences. (White maleness might even stand for difference itself.) This economy has evolved from feminist politics into what is now a socially and culturally induced agenda very difficult to discuss outside occasions almost too specific, narrow, and commonplace. The conceptual power of a categorization such as white maleness is not a single thing or a textual thing. It cannot fairly be represented as either one since it participates in the problematics of such other things as human identity, victimization, intellectual dependency, disciplinary formations, truisms, jobs, politics, and class. I would want to instance this last category especially, only insofar as the "white" of the male marks a racial opposition that stands for class. (How could this be exactly determined? Indeed, the term has power, as so many other culturally loaded terms do, because its action can't be "determined" in some sort of empirical way.) Or rather, the whiteness stands for the anxieties of the great majority of educated whites, men and women both, who have to shore up their social placement continually without explicit reference to those poorer than themselves, so many of whom are black.

Let me consider a passage from Orwell's *The Road to Wigan Pier*, which deals with precisely this conversion of class into race in a manner hard to imagine in the conditions of the present discourse on these matters. Orwell mentions that "the class question appeared at first sight to have been shelved" when he came to Burma as a member of the imperial police. So had the race question. In fact, Orwell says he felt, and still feels, that the Burmese are physically superior. "Compare the firm-knit silken skin of the Burman, which does not wrinkle at all till he is past forty, and then merely withers up like a piece of dry leather, with the coarse-grained, flabby, sagging skin of the white man." Orwell then goes on to suggest how he used this racial difference to mask "my early-acquired class prejudice." He means his fellows stank. "For a soldier is probably as inoffensive, physically, as it is possible for a male white person to be.... But I could not see it like that. All I knew was that it was *lower-class* sweat that I was smelling, and the thought of it made me sick."[11]

The contemporary contrast could not be more complete. First, Orwell's white male has a body. Today's has none. It is an abstract formulation where it is not even more abstractly a rhetorical counter. Second, this male is "white" over against a racial other whose body is even more vividly depicted. Today's black, just so, appears to have even less of a body than any white counterpart, and of course to say anything similar about a black to what Orwell writes of the Burmese would be for an American white the sheerest racism. Third, Orwell's man is "male" in opposition to an other (which even possesses a gender character, since Orwell mentions that he felt toward a Burmese "almost as I felt towards a woman") whose difference from him does not conceal his own division from either himself or from others of his kind. He may have needed the Burmese in order to discover this division. And yet they are not lost in his account merely as a function of Orwell's own identity. Finally, race is understood as a screen for class. Because the natives stand apart from the class system they can be invested with idealism. Yet Orwell makes clear that this idealism is contaminated by class, just as denigration would be.

So what to conclude? Is the manner in which Orwell faces both race and class—and faces them as a white male—to be judged exemplary? Or is it just hard to say why today we'd prefer that he faced gender first (and so it's not easy to read this account and refrain from substituting it for race)? Could the most compelling reason we may have for this preference be that we don't want to face class (except to elide it under gender through race)? In the introduction to his recent collection of essays, *The Invention of Ethnicity*, Werner Sollors states what has become a contemporary credo about how humankind is what it is: "The interpretation of previously 'essentialist' categories (childhood, generations, romantic love, mental health, gender, region, history, biography, and so on) as 'inventions' has resulted in the recognition of the general constructedness of the modern world."[12] This doesn't explain why gender has come to function as, so to speak, the invention of inventions, although it does suggest how there might be some need, as all previously biologized or essentialized categories fall, to keep one uninterpreted as such, and instead effectively given and unconstructed. Nobody has to *say* such a category would make no sense according to the best available intelligence of the human sciences. Everybody should merely agree, for all the best political reasons, on the necessity of reducing such a category to silence, by the principle that it has already spoken quite enough. Consequently white maleness appears to be the last essential category left. And of course the way Orwell *discovers* what he is as a white male becomes something of a theoretical embarrassment.

Finally, the actuality of a white male maintaining some sort of migratory or subversive subjectivity at all may be even more of a scandal to an ideological profile that presumes to have completely comprehended male specificity, notwithstanding its ever-potential ruses. In his well-known strictures on what he calls "women's studies" as having failed to develop structural principles fundamentally different from those they set out to question (and therefore having only "rebuilt the empire of the Law"), Jacques Derrida predicts the following: "Whoever asks questions by definition not coded on these principles of progress risks to appear—in the eyes of women who are activists for women's studies—reactionary, dangerous, only limiting the progress of their positive research" (Jardine and Smith, 193). Henry Louis Gates, Jr., perhaps the most prominent black male critic in the country, cites this very critique in a recent *South Atlantic Quarterly* article and then responds "that the Western male subject has long been constituted historically for himself and in himself." Gates continues: "And, while we readily accept, acknowledge, and partake of the critique of *this* subject as transcendent, to deny us the process of exploring and reclaiming our subjectivity before we critique it is the critical version of the grandfather clause, the double privileging of categories that happen to be *preconstituted*."[13] One subjectivity, it seems, makes itself manifest only by wresting itself free of another, which it declares to be essentialized. Furthermore, if this more powerful subjectivity is that of a (white) male, then a less powerful one is imperiled to recognize it as the subjectivity of subjectivity, whose conditions it, in turn, cannot escape. This is itself a powerful response. Gates would not, I think, content himself with what I have surmised as the scandal of an Orwell—and, instead, would have correctly seen that male subjectivity retains within it the labor of such a self-discovery as Orwell's; indeed, this is why the white male subject is "transcendent"—there simply is no model of any other that does not derive from it.

Does this mean, however, that it is preconstituted? (Especially in our deconstructed moment, when nothing is.) Does it mean, for that matter, that it is exclusionary? Gates, for all his rhetorical moves, does not ultimately take it to be so. His own essay ends with memories of his mother and concludes with an invocation "to speak in the voice of the black female" in order to produce "a discourse of the critical Other" (Gates, "Master's," 111). One of his own recent books mentions the following tension in his own work concerning the racist uses in Western intellectual history of the absence of black writing: "It remains difficult for me to believe that any human being would be demanded to write himself or herself into the human community."[14] Eve Kosofsky Sedgwick, however, expresses a far more familiar assumption about how there appear always to be certain categories of human beings who were written out because they were written up, and so who now have to write themselves back in as if there is no space that awaited them: "Perhaps never again need women—need, one hopes, anybody—feel greeted by the Norton Anthology of mostly white men's literature with the implied insolent salutation, 'I'm nobody. Who are you?'"[15] Not only does this assumption disdain how the literature got socially constructed, has within it its own heterogeneity, suffers its own divisions, acknowledges alternative categories, and even contains its own critique. An assumption such as Sedgwick's merely repeats the same law of the authority she reviles. If Gates, on the other hand, is right, then Sedgwick only passes on the insolence but now without even a gesture of invitation, or inclusion, to any other.

Feminism is part of the law now. The institutional recognition it enjoys is undeniable, even if how this recognition works itself out, day by day, at hundreds of different sites, is extremely difficult to articulate without being anecdotal. (I heard the other day of two colleagues—the sexes have to use a common bathroom in the department—who got into a fight after the woman caught the man in the act of failing to lower the toilet seat and objected, "What about women?" "Why should it be reprehensible for me not to lower it but not for you not to raise it?" the man replied.) Of course it is understandable that women continue to speak of a totality that threatens and oppresses by condensing it in a phrase that incarnates it as a person. Yet this categorization creates—as well as sustains—the conditions of the fear, conditions that are, in part, those of subjectivity itself, female or male. (Sedgwick herself bids to extend the conditions in ways I have discussed as typical of feminist discourse by arguing that the "representational compact" based on the repression of homosexuality be "renegotiated or abrogated" [Segwick, 151].) In a certain real, grimly ironic sense, it has fallen on women and blacks—just as it is now falling on gays—to *make good* the "Western male subject," whether they want to or not. There is no escaping its position or its status; we recall that Lentricchia maintains there is certainly no escaping for men, upon whom the subjectivity confers not so much privilege as responsibility. We could even say there is no escaping the essence of the Western male subject, but only as long as this "essence" is not seen as a biological given, or something unmodified by other differences, or solely the object of discourse rather than also its product.

Certainly the worst thing about being a white male today is that one finds himself more or less a purely consensualized being. While women are mandated to take "the risk of essence" (the oft-cited injunction of Gayatri Spivak), men are accorded no risk and terminal essence. "I know of no form that does not violate the nature of Being in the most unbearable manner," once stated Sammuel Beckett. Is one to take this merely as one of those grandiloquent things Western men have always gotten to say in their happy hegemonic luxuriance? In any case, lots of people know lots of forms. The one of white maleness is a study in how a rigorous formal inquiry can eventually become instrumentalized and bureaucratized, just as those of its energies always most complicit with institutional power licensed it to be. In the feminist critique the impossibility of genderless Being can only be imagined for women, because the remorselessness of gendered Being everywhere continues to be exercised by men.

Do these men take themselves to be white males in exactly the ways they are categorized to be? Who knows? Who knows even after decades of feminist critique about the very grounds of male, if not white male, knowing? It's now common in this critique to read Helene Cixous's injunction that "men still have everything to say about their sexuality" (Cixous, "Laugh," 247).[16] She means apart from women. Yet, even granting that the bad old "scotomizing" terms can be scrapped, how is this saying thence to proceed? In terms of other men? How much can either sex "say" about itself exclusive of the other? I read this Cixous statement as a kind of higher sentimentality. It may be that, for white males, the whole category, as a category, is merely a strange species of otherness—too much like them not to be them, and yet not wholly like them for that. If so, they are then curiously in the position of a black male such as Gates, who criticizes proponents of "Blackness" with the trenchant reply that the word functions as "an entity, rather than as metaphor or sign" (Gates, *Figures*, 39).

How can they say so? They can partially as national beings. As a culture Americans are haunted by categories. Arguably the leading social issue in the United States is how to categorize a fetus, for example. Another: a friend in special education tells me that one of the leading journals in the field has announced a new editorial policy whereby there are no more "mentally retarded persons" but instead "persons with mental retardation." So it goes. We ceaselessly promote some categories, and demote others. We are all Americans, all over again, that "new Man," each time. Unlike fetuses or the mentally retarded, however, white males continue to be capable of participating in the conversation, even if they're repeatedly told that they've been holding forth long enough or that now it's time to listen to what's good for them. One must presume that not all of these men have discovered that they are, or want to be, or should be, women. Who was it who coined the consummate slogan for the 1980s: "Every man for herself!"?

This white male emerges from no such national history and learns nothing from the last decade.[17] How many cultural narratives can continue to be embedded in just one figure? More than one could have guessed a decade ago; the white male has proved capable of providing a remarkably powerful plot—and the tale of homophobic terrors is now one of the newest, and strongest, storylines. How much social tension can be incarnated in one person? Again, more than could have been predicted, once the material social relations that constitute the sexual oppression of women began to become known, addressed, and eased. As a society we persist at being enthralled by the discursive conditions for the very possibility of gender. The power for further knowledge is everywhere, and the example of gay studies suggests how much discursive force is left to be generated and academized. All that appears to remain essential is that some figure—call him transcendent, call him hegemonic, call him *him*, and color him white—function as a locus for power: originary, venerable, representable, and deconstructable. Any man, it seems, will do, although it's best that he's heterosexual and it's only necessary that he's not black.

There's another interesting moment in the concluding conversation between Jardine and Smith at the end of *Men in Feminism*. Smith speaks of the necessity for men now to prove their own specificity, just like women have—something, he adds, that he doesn't think can be done except "through feminism." Jardine won't buy it. She speaks instead of men participating at the "molecular" rather than the "molar" level. She speaks of more "local" strategies. Finally she speaks of not speaking at all. "So do you see *any* efficacy in a politics of silence?" she impatiently pleads with Smith (Jardine and Smith, 257–58). There is more to the conversation but the rest is seduced by silence.

Through feminism, if only in terms of the discretion incumbent upon any form of intellectual inquiry, it's best to conclude that the present is still not the time for a man to wonder about the difference between feeling something and being made to feel it. I take the most obvious lesson of feminism to be, every man for herself. There's probably another just as compelling:

no self at all if somebody doesn't speak for you; it's much too simple to assume that you should "speak for yourself." Of course this business of self-representation remains very hard, and we seem to irritate each other's afflictions pretty much every time we open our gendered mouths, especially in the academy's current more-marginal-than-thou mood. Yet what else is to be done? We can only admit that there are worlds within worlds. There are ones, for instance, where much of what I've been discussing in this essay would be incomprehensible. There are others where all the issues are commonplace. Many—women as well as men—must only resign themselves to the state of affairs in highly individual, haplessly fugitive, and often barely representable ways. We live, each of us, in what Cixous so wondrously terms "the false theater of phallocentric representationalism" (Cixous, 254). It's easier to know what the script is than what to say when you have to open your mouth. For me, one of the most resonant lines was a question given some time ago by Shoshana Felman: "Is it enough to *be* a woman in order to speak as a woman?"[18] Of course it isn't. And it's not enough to be a woman in order to speak about a man. Just so, it's not enough to be a man to be spoken about by a woman.

chapter seven

ON NOT WRITING

A DISSERTATION

THE ARTICLE that follows in the second section of this essay was written twelve years ago. I tried to get it published. I couldn't. One editor pleaded with me, for my own good, not to try anywhere else. Of the rejections, this is the one I remember best. I'm not sure why. Perhaps because this man stated, if not directly, what others took to be the case: that it simply is not in one's professional interest to question the purpose of a dissertation. Somebody has always seemed to know something I didn't, and should have, about dissertations. Where is it written?

I'm not sure much has changed in twelve years. There is no *discourse* about dissertations. At most, there are references—to take an example almost at random, by Eugene Genovese, at the end of his "Acknowledgments" for *Roll, Jordan Roll*, when he mentions that his wife took time from writing her dissertation to help "while under the pressure that anyone who has written a dissertation will readily appreciate." Exactly. Those of us who have been under the obvious, memorable pressure of writing a dissertation will appreciate, understand, forgive. Writing a dissertation is one of the great *acceptable* horrors. Academic life is mute before them: the awful class that just gets worse during the semester, the boring department meeting that becomes more mind-numbing as the afternoon expires. But what would it be like to accept having to write a dissertation, and yet not write it? This is one of the things my original article is about.

Such a case may be no more acceptable now than a decade ago. You may be able to confound or displace the inexorable logic of publish or perish, but it's harder to survive the consequences of writing or not writing a dissertation. What has changed is the disciplinary sophistication about the consequences. At least I read my article now to be engaged less by its careful (not to say painful) self-consciousness than by its astonishing ignorance. I simply did not realize that I was already what today's most theorized idiom might characterize as an "embedded practioneer." Must Stanley Fish any longer always be cited in order to employ oneself the phrase, "interpretive community?" (Part of what one who has done a dissertation "appreciates" is that *not* to cite a known source never ceases to seem a bit illicit.) In any case, that I was a member of such a community was an intelligence utterly unavailable to me twelve years ago. I had not absorbed a poststructuralist critique that assured me that I had not so much a "self" as a "subject position," or that my undissertated condition could be construed as a "site for contestation." I simply failed to see how total is the relationship between cognition and institution. Otherwise, I suppose, I would not have tried to protest that the first can do without the second, much less to protest "in my own name."

Against precisely what was I protesting twelve years ago? In one sense, that I had nothing available to me as a mode of self-description except a negation: I had not done something that I should have done. What the disciplinary strictures of Fish and others now enable me to see is that my situation was not quite this simple. Of course not writing a dissertation is inseparable from the professional imperative to do so in order to enjoy some measure of the fullest possibilities of a career. A dissertation is, moreover, inseparable from a whole ideology of professionalism by which there finally *is* a subject.[1] I had presumed, in other words, at once a too narrow and too naive a conception of myself.

B. L. Reid has a charming memoir, *First Acts*, in which, in a postscript, he briskly records his "tardy" realization ("as I began to think of myself as perhaps the oldest living instructor of English") while teaching at Sweet Briar College in the early 1950s that he was close to the University of Virginia, where he could "get moving on a Ph.D." He does. "It also occurred to me that as my competitive profession honored and rewarded publication, I could turn my course papers, if I were clever and energetic, into publishable essays." He succeeds. That is, he enters into complicity with the constitutive project of professionalism. "I was always an impressionist, an appreciator, a chronic student," concludes Reid.[2] What he fails to realize is that his decision to work toward his doctorate is what permits him to sustain this "always," just as his impressions would lack coherence without a Ph.D. or his student analogy would have been impossible to maintain without tenure (which he is offered, from Mount Holyoke, when, at age 39, he completes his doctorate). Indeed, professionalism is what empowers Reid to make the ideological move whereby he can present himself beyond either the arbitrary specializations of the discipline or the grimmer rigors of any ideology.

So, at any rate, goes the present critique: there are only the norms and constraints of the discipline, and one is never more bound by them than when one takes oneself to be breaking free, because such action has no coherence apart from them. But what am I to assume now about my own case? Merely that I represented an unintelligible personal instance in having failed to write a dissertation? Or perhaps that I have now a mode of self-description available that in fact enables an affirmation, albeit not of me, but of the professional practice that accords me whatever "site" I possess from which meaningfully to contest anything at all? But wouldn't this be like finding that the worst victims of anything suffer from lack of definition, or that the best opponents ultimately celebrate the structures that frame them? What does one do with outmoded subjectivity?

There is no discourse about the writing of dissertations in part because there is no discourse about what it means to have failed to write one. I will have more to say about this in my third section. Let me content myself at this point with the following disciplinary assessment of dissertation writing: the practice can now be relegitimated as one phase in a continuum of professional behavior that may be represented, or otherwise reformulated, without questioning its rationale or in any way unsettling its necessity. So, for example, one can read that it now takes more time for students to earn the doctorate and that more fail to do so. The "subject position" remains in place. One can learn that in the sciences and engineering something known as "stapling" a dissertation (assembling a collection of published articles) now constitutes a valid option for submission. The "site of contestation" is not radically energized. Nobody appears to inquire whether dissertations should be done at all, at what cost they continue to be required, or if they disable the scholarly futures of far more people than they enable because they now take longer to write than ever.

Especially in a discipline such as English, where all who are called except to the most elite institutions must file past the omnivorous, many-sectioned monster of composition, how many are going to have scholarly futures anyway? A dissertation is popularly waved along as a "rite of passage." If you want to get promoted, get recognized, or just get paid, you have to get on with it and get through it. Everybody knows this. A profession is a profession as much because of what "everybody knows" as because it has its rites. A professional gets to be a professional by submitting to both. There is no sort of profession, nor any sort of professional, apart from the knowledge that binds and the ceremonies that sanction. Reid may have been exceptional, and it may have been undeniably unfortunate that he could have languished as an instructor forever at Sweet Briar had he not become resolute for a Ph.D. Yet a profession without rigorous, hierarchical standards for credentializing lacks authority. If you want to move up in it, you play its game. What else is there to say?

This brings me back to what I wrote twelve years ago. If you fail to write a dissertation, my feeling is that you will forever return to the conditions of that failure. Indeed, it may be that even many who succeed in writing one never quite forget its obligatory trauma. (I have a friend whose own dissertation was so easy that to this day he refuses to talk about it, as if he committed a crime.) My article still stands for me as an attempt to express the haunting, obsessive nature of the experience of, arguably, the most impeccably *imposed* writing it is possible for anyone to have to try to do. In this sense, my theoretical naïveté, as I now understand it, seems to me more instructive in itself than anything I could try to write today.

Of course I wouldn't try to write anything today about not having written a dissertation. The most uninterestingly factual reason why must be trusted to survive a number of other reasons that it will be the burden of this chapter to set out, first, in a third section, and then more decisively in a fourth. Such an organization is bound to appear fussy and muffled. I can't avoid it. I'm not writing fiction. I probably ought to be writing comedy. I take myself to be partaking probably a bit too much of the first, and not nearly enough of the second in order to recuperate a species of remorseless subjectivity that doesn't very easily command any secure formal dispensation. My argument will be that there is no discourse about writing a dissertation because there is no subjectivity granted to the process. A dissertation is, so to speak, all purpose. The institutional *fact* of a dissertation: it sloughs off all temporizing emotions, uses up all ambiguities, and throws over all protestations. (Like any ritual, it purges subjectivity and renders what must be undergone as something impersonal.) And when at last completed, a dissertation must be immediately abandoned *as such;* "no unrevised dissertations considered," publishers caution. Why the caution? Is it because, in addition, a dissertation is ultimately nothing but the sum of its discipline, ceremony, and form?

What I propose to do here, on the contrary, is to offer an account of not writing a dissertation as a condition that has persisted for me beneath discipline, apart from ceremony, and despite form. I give the account first, in the next section, with my original subjectivity intact, and then, in the following two, with revisions. The revisions exist in part because of the drama of adding them—and therefore opening up the gaps in which the profession has such a theoretical investment. Furthermore, the revisions express in part my additional theoretical authorization to locate some recuperative value—if only because of what it might illuminate, now, about a discipline's central legitimating practice. And, finally, revisions, each neatly sectioned, are here because I do believe that publishers are right to caution authors of dissertations about submitting them unrevised. A dissertation is not a book. A dissertation is like nothing else. A dissertation, in the most fundamental sense, is what it is because it is a writing that awaits its revisions; interred as only a dissertation, it awaits redemption as a book. By the same logic, in my case, writing about not having written a dissertation didn't suffice; it only abided, I now see, until, years later, I can once again consider more fully and deliberately how the very fact of a dissertation has inescapably become probably the most irredeemable fact of my career.

2

ON NOT HAVING WRITTEN A DISSERTATION

> *I don't care about myself, but save my doctoral dissertation.*
> —David Lodge, The British Museum is Falling Down, *(during a fire alarm)*

A couple of years ago I attended a party given by a member of an English department at a prominent eastern university. I met another man there who had his doctorate from the same university I had attended as a graduate student and who had been there a couple of the same years as me, though we never knew each other. At one point he was bemoaning the spiritlessness of his graduate classes. I remarked that I'd be glad to have them, especially since I'd never taught a graduate class. "Well," he snapped, as if detecting a whine of self-pity, "you never finished your dissertation, did you?"

Indeed I had not. My writtens, yes, and my orals as well, but not my dissertation, as I had mentioned to him. I didn't mention it to the graduate students I talked to at the party, some working on dissertations. I was surprised that none tried to strike attitudes, uneasy or aloof, to me, possessor of a job as I was, but it discomfited me nevertheless to realize that even the best of them, "dissertation in hand" (as the MLA vacancy lists may still say), would be lucky to get the sort of position I already had, and had kept, without the dissertations they strove to finish in order to be considered for a position at all. There is, I suspect, no small measure of guilt (for lack of a better word) that tenured, dissertationless people such as myself might well feel before such students—comfortably nestled inside the walls as we are and yet lacking the full credentials even to be permitted to approach the gate.

Such a residence, for me anyway, has not been without its uneasy moments. The first time a student asked me if he should call me "Doctor," I took some pleasure in sneering, "I don't give a damn." But it was a cheap, hypocritical pleasure, born out of the contradiction between the wish I could just say "yes" and the conviction that it didn't matter anyway. I used to receive a casual, "Hi, Dr. Caesar," in a lighter, if no purer spirit, but soon that came to be sullied by various kinds of ironic amusement, and by now my feeling has dried up into indifference. These days, you're lucky to get a friendly greeting rather than a muttered curse anyway. I think I told the last student who asked how he should address me the story a colleague once told me of the German professor who beat a student out of his office with a cane for entering it and addressing him as "Herr Professor." "Herr Doctor Professor" was of course the proper form.

Among others in the profession I have met over the years from outside my own institution my, er, deficiency has usually been archly regarded where it was known, and often single-mindedly suspected where it was not. I remember especially a woman in an NEH Summer Seminar with me a few years ago. She *knew*; her own dissertation was of too great significance for her not to know. (A member of my department had cried out in the main office, "But I thought you had to have a Ph.D!" when he learned I'd gotten the award.) When she finally asked me directly the sheer fact of the scandal was too overpowering, and she recoiled in horror and disbelief at my affirmative reply: "Oh, oh, *Oh* . . ." Others, of course, have indicated no particular concern, when they cared to ask. Two years ago I visited a man I hadn't seen since graduate school, when we'd been office mates for a year. He was brilliant, and to term him a rebel would only be to slight the passion with which he held his convictions and the courage with which he lived his life. He'd written his dissertation too. "I never wrote it," I said, when he asked, and he cried, "Great!" In my own experience, and the official views of department chairmen quite aside, I suppose these two identities—interloper and rebel—cover the spectrum of attitudes; the rest may have been temperate, or tempered, to the point of hardly being manifest at all.

Of any of them, that "Great!" delighted me most, but it came too late. Years had passed. Defined by not having done something, I could no longer convert it into something else that I had instead accomplished. Besides, not having a dissertation had long since become less a matter of my relations with others than my relations with myself. The first chairman I had, whose semiannual inquiries into the progress of the thing ("Does the library have all the books you need?") once made me squirm with dissembling and cringe with failure, was gone. What little direct pressure I had from my institution to complete my degree had long since ceased. "We're supposed to teach literature, not literacy," a friend moaned one day, and indeed: the latter has never seemed more imperative, the former more redundant—or rather the training that comprises the "terminal degree" and the act of scholarship that crowns it.

Termination: much as I want to sneer at the word, it is precisely this that I have denied myself, and it's a denial I still feel. Less a deprivation than a vacancy, perhaps, for not having written a dissertation has been to have to acknowledge the perpetual presence of an absence. Not so much something not done as something not *accomplished*. Insofar as I've longed for the inevitable pride of a task completed, over, and done, I've experienced instead the ignominy merely of an expectation, and one not met because expected of me (though it was) but because I came to expect it of myself. Certainly the reasons why the completion of a dissertation is still held to be mandatory for the reception of a doctorate no longer interest me and never really did. Compromised anyway, I never wished to decry the necessity, whose justification now seems to me to have eroded to little more than the status of a last threshold beyond which departments can begin sorting out candidates for jobs on quite other bases. These remain as wayward and arbitrary as ever, but as the "terminal degree" certifies the expiration of one period in the life of the mind presumably it also functions to insure the hope that without this death no more mature intelligence will be reborn.

"For the last time psychology."—Kafka. I still wonder if I didn't secretly resist this rebirth and want instead the irony of so regarding it. Did I deliberately choose a subject entirely new to me despite the advice of others that that's the most foolish thing one can do? Did I want more than anything else the assurance that what I would write would be worth doing, while I saw others scurrying away with the letters of Brete Harte or the novels of Brian Moore? The years have worn away the grudgingness with which I came to admit that I simply had nothing new or worthwhile to contribute to the study of W. B. Yeats. But was this a defense of the value of scholarship or an attack on it? An admission of pride or a recognition of frailty? Certainly I've taken pride in the fact that I spent the best part of the year I should've been writing reading instead in philosophy and anthropology, subjects I had no time for until my courses were completed. But I also spent the worst part of that year dutifully groping through every known work on Yeats and accumulating notes as if for visible proof of my endeavor, whereas in fact such doggedness only dispersed my concentration and displaced the energy I should've used to establish my own focus. (Graduate students now, with bleaker job prospects than I had to face, must watch the note cards mount with even more bitterness and barely suppressed futility.) The poem, Valery said, is never finished, only abandoned. The only pleasure I take looking back over this year now is that I never really got started writing and abandoned what little I had written as soon as I began teaching. Except for a summer two years later, I never picked it up again, and was (dis)content to ply my own vacuities quite apart from the rigors of the actual struggle with words.

To write a dissertation is (I think) above all to subject yourself to the process of writing a dissertation. It is not, or not simply, the writing. From such bondage comes freedom—say for more mature scholarly tasks to come, now yours rightly, demonstrably, to aspire to; in some cases, yours manifestly already. The fact that this does not necessarily happen; the fact that more often than not the process only succeeds in using up the knowledge and the skills it (putatively) serves both to validate and to free; the fact does not matter. The great thing is to go through the motions. A dissertation exists as something *to have done*.

But not having done it, I am still not insensitive (as the British might say) to the spirit of the thing. Indeed, it sometimes seems to me (and more so now that to think about it becomes detached from the need to justify, and to contemplate failure simply becomes the acceptance of a fate) that I have written my dissertation—nay, lived the writing of it—more thoroughly, deeply, and perhaps even richly than if I had actually written it. I would claim the agonies and tremors of the process as much as any who have seen them through to conclusion. The *idea* of writing a dissertation has adhered to my life more, perhaps (and "perhaps" is a word that one needs to have available for writing a dissertation) than most who have (it seems almost a vulgar thought) *dispensed* with it. I have felt the purity and the force of that idea the more for never having let it dwindle into words. I think of Valery once again, who used to look in every illustrious book for the error that caused it to be known. But a dissertation, in itself, is a dim thing and seldom either seeks or achieves the glare of public view, much less the harsh radiance of centuries. Mine will never be known, and not even I will ever know the error by which it could've come into existence. Not to have written it often strikes me now as a finer truth.

It is a truth that has no authority, however. Certainly not the authority that would enable me to teach a graduate course at a prominent eastern university. Nor is it a truth that really has the means to reveal itself. Not having written a dissertation is defined as the failure to have done something, and failure has no voice, or no reply.

Some time ago a friend who has left teaching joked that he wished he could give me his doctorate since he didn't need it anymore. He received it at the same institution where I could've received mine. He finished his dissertation while teaching at another school, but his department still refused him tenure. The joke struck me as funnier than it should have, in a sort of hollow, intellectual way. I wondered if I could accept his offer, if such a thing were possible. I decided I could not. Not only because I would've had to deny my sort of perpetual rediscovery of the conditions for writing a dissertation; not only because I would've had to efface a continual forbearance about the significance of having done so; but simply because not having written a dissertation has become as equivalent to me as having lived. And if there is a life, so to speak, that is no less a life for never having been lived, there is the writing that is equally inscribed for never having been written.

3

There is no subjectivity without its tones. Few things dissatisfy me now more than mine. There are too many, ranging from the jocular to the formal and severe. The Lodge epigraph represents a species of sweet comedy that I couldn't command. Two of the last three paragraphs get too arch in order to try to avoid being disingenuous, and I think it is at last in these where I fail to swing free of the self-pity anyone who knew told me I'd never avoid if I so much as tried to write on this subject.

There is no subjectivity without its outside. If only in order to avoid sounding choked, I was never sure what else to include. Many of the graduate students mentioned in the second paragraph, for example, have subsequently become the part-time teachers who have, in turn, given the discipline a substantially different profile than twelve years ago, when tenure-track positions defined it far more. Furthermore, what I later referred to as "literacy" has since been more rigorously defined by the field of composition studies, whose theoretical ambitions perhaps ought to have been more obvious to me even twelve years ago. But how much was I implicated in such developments even then? And how cynical to suggest now that part-time teaching on a massive scale is one clear way to take care of many prospective professionals who are going to spend most of their time teaching three and four sections of composition per semester and so who don't really need to write dissertations?

I'm not sure I'd have written anything about not having a dissertation had I known some of the horror stories I eventually heard. To take one example: a woman had finished her dissertation at one of the best universities in the country, but its director died before it was approved by departmental committee. The archenemy of her director was appointed as her new director. He demanded a complete rewrite. Years have passed now. This woman still doesn't want to admit that she'll never do a dissertation. Another example: a man finished his dissertation in record time—four months, I think—but a member of his committee demanded it be redone because one of its basic ideas was completely unacceptable to him. This idea was, in turn, the reason a portion of the dissertation had already gotten published (in another country). Nonetheless, my man had to rewrite the whole thing, even though he almost had a nervous breakdown because he only learned of the judgment less than a week before his defense. Compared to such stories, my own unwritten condition looks to me awfully routine now, preciously inward and even luxuriantly meditated. And I never even considered the defense (the best date, the right committee members, and so on) that is now arguably equally an obstacle to the Ph.D. degree as the dissertation itself. Lately, I've heard a lot of defense stories. Is it just that candidates and professors both are getting older and more rigid?

Of course plenty of people go through doctoral desiderata successfully each year. Do they reveal more than those who aren't successful the blunt fact of professional hegemony itself?[3] The knowledge researched, organized, and displayed by a dissertation confirms that it is all esoteric enough to seal, each time, a discipline's authority. Who groans more under this authority, and thereby better discloses its sway? Or are complaints about writing a dissertation merely part of the ritual? (Even if it's "going well," it's usually better not to say so, especially very enthusiastically, and especially to friends who haven't finished their own dissertations.) Complaints are just personal, have no conceptual status, and exhaust themselves in any case once the last page of the thing is written, if not when the last approving comment is made by a committee. The point about the routine is that it can *only* be successful; otherwise, it has no more existence than an irresponsible director or an unprincipled reader—or an unwritten dissertation.

To put this another way: there is only one story to a dissertation, the official one, success. Embedded, or rather impacted, within this story may be any number of others: intolerable drudgery, humiliating subservience, ideas lost to "scholarship," or scholarship aspiring to ideas. (I have another friend who at last gained entrance to her languid adviser's home, only to have them both discover that his infant daughter had urinated all over the chapter he was supposed to have read.) None of these matters. What might be called the *unwritten* either gets into or stays away from the writing. It doesn't survive it.[4] Afterwards, perhaps, someone might want to write about the writing, and yet the possibility seems to me to be superfluous to the enacted routine, at once too complete and too decisive in itself—which is, after all, again, its point.

The trouble with my article is that it has no story to tell, only a consciousness, variously deployed, about how my not having written a dissertation has had to writhe before the clear, legitimized outline of the official narrative. Related plots I inscribe only to dismiss. Some sort of heroism based on broad knowledge rather than narrow specialization I never really consider. Some sort of significance in terms of teaching rather than publication I only suppress. The most obvious role of rebel gives me no consolation. By the end, there is space for nothing else but failure. In trying to transform it into a higher vein of success, I think I finally but acknowledge the force—if not the terms—of the official story.[5] I didn't do something. The most I can say is that I've lived it, I've never lived past it, I've never forgotten.

Does this subjectivity possess any theoretical authority? In one sense, no, especially since I am never exempt from—indeed, as I have emphasized earlier, am instead constituted by—the values and principles of the discipline. Yet, in another sense, yes, I think my subjectivity does have theoretical interest, and this is precisely because I am not exempt from institutionalized imperatives. I have already rehearsed the current professionalist critique: as professionals, we are always already in place, and there is no truth or value apart from the professional enterprise, which defines any choices that could be made, because they cannot be made somehow abstracted from the institutional context. In exactly such terms, I stated no claim to be in any way abstracted. I never *denied* the dissertation. I simply didn't do it. Instead, I wore myself out trying to cleanse my motives for not doing it until I had to acknowledge that they were contaminated by various professional mandates that I couldn't get rid of. In the process, I could only reproduce these mandates inside myself through a labor of extenuation that was never in a constant relation to them. Writing the article only succeeded in misrepresenting this relation by making it appear more constant than it was. There were long periods of time, for example, when I didn't give a dissertated damn. The only scriptable space I had was that for something unwritten. What theory is there for that?

Or rather, what profession? What if the difference between something written and something not is not an absolute one? Moreover, if I claim now that my relation to the significance of the dissertation was not as constant as I had written it to be, is this not a way of demonstrating that I could not *represent* the subject at all? How to, as it were, *accredit* such questions? The way I would do so now is to situate my text of twelve years ago as a demonstration of how something not done can abide as *interior* to a discipline that recognizes only the outward accomplishment. I had abided—tenured and promoted, no less—but these things didn't matter so much. In not writing a dissertation, I in effect exchanged a closed, external occasion for an open, inward one and thereby exposed the certifiable fact of having written a dissertation to more insecurities, contingencies, accidents, and duplicities than it was ever designed to accommodate. The profession has no name for this. So I didn't either.

In other words, it's not that my writing was heedless of disciplinary context. Instead, I'd taken myself to exist as it were posterior to this context, or anyway long past the one occasion—writing a dissertation—that remained for me the most urgent way of ratifying any relation at all that I had to the profession. One clear take that I have on my article now is as an agonized example of the dissertation's authority in the profession. Another, however, is far more interesting: as an unaccommodated instance of how this very authority can be emptied out. In the name of what? Not something larger or higher. More modestly, I think, merely in the name of a human agency that insists it could have done otherwise. Furthermore, an agency that insists that its own careful enunciation of what it didn't do amounts to an incarnated, faithful labor of its own. (I don't know why I didn't quote Yeats: "Man can embody truth. He cannot know it." I suppose I was embarrassed at such a spiritual idiom.) This is of course all very paradoxical. The profession of English has always honored paradoxes. The trick is sometimes to conceal them by turning them into strategies.

Not writing a dissertation wasn't a strategy for me, however. Nor was it a project. The years passed, and it assumed the character of something I did actually do, not something I failed to do. The years passed, and it was almost as if I came to feel my career was a testimony to the crucial importance of this last distinction, the logical nonsense be damned of not doing something transformed anyway into a doing. Perhaps this is one reason I finally wrote about not having written a dissertation—to test the logic.

There was, however, another reason, and I want to devote a final section of this paper to it: in fact, I must confess, I had just written a dissertation. Or rather, I had completed a manuscript that was eventually accepted as a dissertation. I didn't know this would be the case the night twelve years ago when I wrote about not having written a dissertation, almost immediately after finishing the manuscript's last page. It had taken some seven months to get to this page. Yet, that night, it was as if I'd written to get there only in order to write a few pages about not having written a dissertation. In addition, I wrote as if to prove that, even in committing what I hoped by then, admittedly, would be a dissertation, I had continued to live past the disciplinary context for doing so. The degree didn't matter. Writing a dissertation, like not writing one, was merely something I had done, just as not writing one was merely something I didn't do.

4

On not writing a dissertation: twelve years after having turned out to have written one, many of the securities of which I'd deprived myself before are now nameable—writable, authorized. I've taught many graduate classes, for example, and I've published quite a few articles (several based on my dissertation—the classic pattern). But I keep returning to the night in which I wrote about not doing what I in fact had just finished doing.

I can't remember now how much, that night, I really hoped my manuscript would indeed prove to be a dissertation. I'd had no contact with my university. My former dissertation director could be dead for all I knew. The only reason I'd written anything is because I'd been awarded a sabbatical for a year. My official reason? To "finish my dissertation"—something I put down just to get the time off, and only afterwards found to stand atop selection criteria for faculty that year. After a month or so traveling in England, I suddenly came to a full realization of how unusually favorable my circumstances were to do research, and soon I was absorbed. As months passed, notecards turned into pages, and chapters accumulated. I believe I was only fitfully aware that I was writing something that I could conceivably submit as a dissertation, if some deadline hadn't passed. I don't remember caring much about this. What I was doing fascinated me. I loved it. I don't even remember thinking that if what I was writing could get accepted as a dissertation, it would have turned out that I had been enjoying, in one sense, an ideal state—a sort of professional bracketing—for the writing.

In another sense, and one far more interesting, this state partook of the duplicitous professional context (at once present and absent, saturated and depleted) that had simply become my very life. I was writing because I was a practioneer in a discipline. In addition, I was at my desk as a member of an institution's faculty. My ostensible mandate was of the most unexceptionable professional kind. Yet what I was doing continued beneath all these names; even if it could be eventually designated as a "dissertation," I was undoubtedly only writing because I felt utterly free from the nomination. Moreover, what I subsequently came to understand—and phrase—about my years prior to this writing as a "perpetual rediscovery of the conditions for writing a dissertation" now felt during this year as nothing more than another phase of the rediscovery; curious, I mused (when? how many times?) that one condition, this present one, should have revealed itself as one in which a dissertation—or at least something suspiciously like it—could issue forth as if I'd never actually *begun* it at all.

How to explain this now? Could it actually have been that I

was more purged of grasping professional motive twelve years ago than I ever could have admitted before I tried to write of it? There are too many coils of consciousness. I think I wrote about not having written a dissertation the first chance I got in order to assure myself that, no, I was not purged. How could I have been? The significance of a dissertation retained for me as much coercive force as I'd previously believed it did. What I wrote that night proved it, and probably disproved some claim on the part of what I'd been doing the past seven months to the title of "dissertation."

Or did it? To state, twelve years later, that I'm not sure, is to admit that I'll never know. To state I'm not sure is now equivalent to saying that I no longer care. Certainly something vital about my motives—personal as well as institutional—had gotten *lost* in the dissertation. (It took some five months before it was officially decreed by the university that my writing was eligible to be so designated.) This frightened me. As I wrote, I kept a separate notebook in which I recorded various stray thoughts—as if I wanted to preserve somehow in the writing another narrative, perhaps one of self-discovery, perhaps just one that could never be represented in any way by what I was writing. It may only sound glibly disaffiliated now to claim that one distinct purpose was, if not precisely to avert writing a dissertation, at least to register within it something incomplete or in need of supplement. If you're left long enough with something in lieu of something else, how long before you'll have everything you need?

Yet there is a limit to subjectivity, to self-knowledge, to intention, to disciplinary authority—and a limit to what something unwritten does when it gets into something written. Do we write in order to remove existing names or to create new ones? Before we can create new ones, must we remove existing ones? Could the removal itself be the new inscription? It will come as no surprise for me to state that the subject of my dissertation was parody.

Although I began my study with Victorian parody, all that

I wrote circled about my fascination with a question and a statement. The question is Roland Barthes's in *S/Z*, at the conclusion of a long meditation on what he terms "a multivalent text." This text flouts the respect due such things as origin and propriety; it even abolishes quotation marks. Therefore it is parodic, and so Barthes asks the following: "What could a parody be that did not advertise itself as such?"[6] He doesn't stay for an answer. He doesn't have to. He is studying, among other things, how subversion begins with the Proper Name, and how, today, the Proper Name is obsolete. On the other hand, I had to stay. If I wanted to write a dissertation, I had to. Even a dissertation on parody has to advertise itself "as such." Indeed, what other writing endures the exquisite formal constraints of the "as such" so faultlessly as a dissertation?

The statement is something I first read attributed to William Empson. So I attributed it to him in my dissertation, and eventually found both the right book and the right page number. The page doesn't make clear, however, whether the words were written by Swift. I liked this undecidability even better. I never mentioned it in my dissertation. Nobody noticed. I just quoted the words: "Everything spiritual and valuable has a gross and revolting parody, very similar to it. Only unremitting judgment can distinguish between them." Maybe so, maybe they can be so distinguished. One doesn't readily argue with Empson (or Swift)—and never in a dissertation. There must be all honor to the profession, including its canonical figures, in a dissertation. A dissertation one just writes. It's better not to think much about it. Alas, I have. But I still don't quite know what to think about the gross fact that I wrote mine.

chapter eight

ON TEACHING AT A

SECOND-RATE UNIVERSITY

A WHILE AGO the chairman of the English department at Clarion University (formerly Clarion State College) of Pennsylvania received a letter of application to the graduate program from a Chinese student, which said in part: "Your college has a long history and a fine tradition of scholarship. It is well staffed and equipped, enjoying world-wide fame. To find a place in such an ideal school of higher learning is indeed a matter of the highest honour." How to respond to these words? Clarion, founded in 1867, doesn't have an especially long history for an American college, and it has no tradition at all for scholarship. Furthermore, it has no national, much less international, fame. The poor Chinese student, we might feel, haplessly writes out of his own rhetorical conventions. Ours are more realistic, and our universities are not all famous.

And yet consider the following comment by Clarion's new president-to-be, when asked, by the student newspaper, what "sparked her interest" in Clarion: "I decided to apply due to the academic reputation. I did know it has a nice, strong reputation. As I became involved in the search process, I began to realize what the special qualities of Clarion are. I think Clarion has a great future." Of course these words are different from those of the Chinese student. The new president would not be so foolish as to claim that Clarion has a global reputation. She is not even so foolish as to risk stipulating where it is exactly that Clarion has any reputation, beyond, presumably, a few hundred miles in any direction (from within such a circumference, in fact, the woman herself was chosen). Most important, she does not say precisely what this "academic" reputation is. And yet, is not the new president expressing a more knowing version of what the Chinese student claims? That is, Clarion is at least not without what one might call its "fame." Consequently, it is a fate not without honor for a person to find a place there.

It may indeed be such a fate. The first thing to say about teaching at a second-rate university, however, may be the last thing: it actually has no reputation at all. Even its local one is a form of name recognition more than anything else. To be employed at such an institution is continually to have to witness the gap that opens up between how its situation might be accurately described and how it is described for public consumption. The only problem with this gap in turn is that, theoretically, it has no language available to it. No second-rate university is going to describe itself as second-rate. Any language used is derived from that suitable for first-rate institutions, which possess reputations either so secure or so widespread that they don't have to lay on the rhetoric for every conceivable occasion. Would the same Chinese student feel his formulas so necessary if he were applying to, say, Princeton? Certainly the same president-to-be would not give the same assurances if she were about to ascend to the presidency of, say, Dartmouth, or Kenyon College, or perhaps even Lenoir-Rhyne or the University of Idaho. But with these last two the idea of a first-rate institution may be stretched too thin. The gap, like the judgment: is it merely subjective? Unjustifiable?

The difference between my own university as it abides in me and as it is evaluated by others yawns for me anyway in ways that make the international rhetoric even more difficult to distinguish from the local. Someone recently showed me a letter from an Indian student to the dean of the graduate school that concluded as follows: "I will encounter stiff competition from all those desiring to pursue a M.A. degree in English at Clarion University. If I have the honour of being chosen from among the teeming multitude vying for a seat, I promise that I will live up to your confidence in me." This struck me as more touching than the praise offered by the Chinese student, and, in a way, more painful, since the program actually accepts virtually any American student so that it will not have to choose between either accepting too many foreign students or letting the program be canceled by the administration for lack of a sufficient "multitude."

Compare the estimation in the interim president's letter to the English department (concerning yet another squabble over the election of a chairperson): "You have our heartfelt best wishes as you seek to preserve those things which should be preserved, to change those things which should be changed, and to keep Clarion University's Department of English at the forefront of your profession." Again, for me this is more touching—not to say pathetic—than the words of his successor, I think because the president's phrasings are as naively mannered as those of a high-school principal. Or maybe the gap here is just more moving because the department is so hopelessly at the rear of the profession that it's still discovering how to sit up.

In any case, after such knowledge, what comedy? It may be

the fundamental experience of teaching at a second-rate university that it is either very serious or very funny, without any allowable or manageable possibility in between. What is it like at a first-rate institution? At such an institution, does the student newspaper print, as mine last year did, the reflections of a senior on The Meaning of It All: "I think a major stepping stone in my sophomore year came when I actually found the desire to open up a newspaper. That's when my mind opened." I don't know. I've never taught at a first-rate institution. It may be the case, in its second-rate heart of hearts, that there are depths at second-rate institutions where knowledge of its subordinate relation with institutions higher, or finer, or more renowned, just falls away and there is nothing, and need be nothing, but the givens of a woefully provincial student body and an irremediably mediocre faculty. It is certainly one thing to be second-rate, another thing to *remain* so.

I'm not sure that Clarion has tried hard enough, but I would not want to claim that Clarion has some special distinction in this or any regard. I merely mean to consider it as a typical second-rate institution. One of fourteen Pennsylvania state system universities (all of which were mandated into existence when the system was created in 1983), Clarion is adequately enough set out in a little statement on a folder from Continuing Education: "a multi-purpose institution with an enrollment of 5200 students [which] offers associate degrees in three areas; more than 60 baccalaureate programs . . . and 12 graduate programs. . . . It is the goal of the University to offer high quality educational programs staffed by excellent faculty within a learning environment in which the rights of all people are respected." In other words, there are smaller universities (and Clarion has grown to over six thousand in recent years) that for all I know advertise themselves as being single-purpose, which don't award associate degrees, not in three areas, and have no graduate programs.

Second-rateness is not solely a matter of variety of programs or size, although each of these helps. (It would be interesting to study which of the "Comprehensive Institutions"—in which Clarion is a member and so categorized by the American Association of University Professors rating scale—can be recognized as having some measure of distinction in terms of the doctoral institutions rated above them.) Arguably, it's not strictly a matter of provinciality or mediocrity, although each of these helps even more. (One of the few truly exceptional students I've had went on to graduate school at Johns Hopkins. "Where you goin'—John Hancock?" one of his friends asked. I'm not sure whether this friend was one of the 57 percent whose verbal SATs are under 500.) Second-rateness is ultimately a matter, more than anything else, of perception. I believe it was an Israeli poet who once said that "the difference between me and Auden is that I have to be aware of him, whereas he doesn't have to be aware of me." The second-rate always has to be aware of some greater measure of anything distinguished, from which its own lesser measure is derived. Not to be so aware—that is, to proceed in either hapless or wilful ignorance that one is all by oneself "at the forefront"— is probably the surest way for an institution to remain second rate.

And if one doesn't choose to remain ignorant, what consolation? Once I had the opportunity to represent the institution at a graduate fair in Washington, D.C. Each school shared a table with another. Clarion's neighbor was Johns Hopkins, specifically its vastly celebrated School of Advanced International Studies program. So many prospective students crowded in front of the table in their desire to get information about this program that Clarion literally was not visible. (Three students did step up to say hello, each one a Clarion graduate surprised and delighted to see "good ole Clarion" there at all.) Eventually I began giving out advice on SAIS in order to help the Hopkins staff with the overflow. But it was too embarrassing. I left an hour early. Not, however, before taking lots of SAIS information. I'd gotten so excited about the program I wanted to consider applying myself. Sometimes there is no consolation.

Or else there is, as always, only it's comedy. A former colleague loved to tell the story of how, during a golden summer as a member of an NEH summer seminar at Stanford, he once had the opportunity to meet one of the most distinguished members of the profession at a party. The man was quite old. Just before my colleague was introduced to him, a member of the seminar from Montana State was introduced. "You could see he'd never *heard* of Montana. The poor old guy was getting exhausted at having to respond to all these places he'd never heard of." So when the next person stepped up and was identified as being from "Clarion University of Pennsylvania," my colleague just nodded in silent assent as the distinguished scholar hopefully queried, "Penn?" I remembered this story, and shrugged unprotestingly myself, years later, when I was designated as being from Penn on the occasion of a lecture at the American Cultural Center in Cairo. Is every second-rate school representable so neatly as a caricature of itself? Or, if so, does the representation only function in such personal, anecdotal ways?

There is no *discourse* publicly about such matters in American higher education. Everybody knows that there is a difference between a Clarion and a University of Pennsylvania. By knowing that difference, however, what precisely does everybody know, and what does it mean in daily, experiential terms to know it? It matters who is doing the knowing; the Israeli's point about Auden is one of the most profound assessments I know, and yet undoubtedly Auden had to know much, for his own part (including perhaps his own complaints at being wrongly or insufficiently known), that the Israeli could not easily imagine. (My own experience simply hasn't given me enough knowledge of people at the country's most prestigious institutions who hated the competition, were chilled by the insatiable drives toward individual recognition, and just opted out, sour grapes be damned.) What matters at least as much, I believe, is that everyone pretty much proceeds as if a Clarion and a Penn merely continue along the paths of their admittedly separate "missions," each relatively unaffected by the other and pleased to be so, if only because ultimately what each does is all of a piece.[1] As it is, the one can be forgiven, and the other thanked, for not mentioning that the most decisive relation between them is the domination of the one by the other. Clarions have no prestige; Penns do. Part of what follows because Penns do, and dominate because they do, is that to try to speak of this prestigelessness at all from the dominated position is to appear to be protesting the inescapable fact of distinction itself; there is a real sense in which it is, after all, no more remarkable that some institutions have more prestige than others than that some people have more money or that some areas have better weather.

Must any attempt to register the domination be relegated to a species of protest? Must any sort of contention over the very fact of distinction seem foolish? For me, teaching at a second-rate university has meant having a professional life rich with such questions. For example, in 1989, unconsoled and unamused, I requested application materials for a Woodrow Wilson Fellowship by writing a letter that included the following paragraph:

> To be quite blunt about it: what are the chances of someone who applies from an institution with the above letterhead actually being awarded a fellowship? Just about nil, I'd say. You know it. I know it. Now you know I know it. But you're not going to tell me you know it in a written statement. Fair enough. You will want to tell me instead about pluralistic aims, humanistic goals, fair practices, and so on. But please don't tell me all this. What I don't know is the record of people who have actually been awarded fellowships over the course of, say, the last ten years. If anyone from an institution as undistinguished as mine has ever been awarded a fellowship, then I'll think very seriously about applying. I've already got a good proposal. But it would play better from Princeton.

What I received, along with the materials, was a list of scholars in residence for that year: such places as Duke, Rice, and the University of Washington were all very predictably predominant. The most hopeful reply to my question that I could find was one man from the State University of New York at New Paltz. He was the dean of liberal arts and sciences. I didn't apply.

More interesting was a complete list of fellows and associates of the National Humanities Center for the years 1978 to 1989. Therein can be discerned an occasional Oberlin College, rather like the one Carleton and the one Colby from the Woodrow Wilson list. In addition, there were two institutions I'd never heard of, Morgan State University and Warren Wilson College, as well as two more, the University of Maine at Farmington and Penn State University at Shenango, which were both most heartening. Indeed, to my astonishment, there was actually one award to a woman from West Chester, the largest university in the Pennsylvania state system. These last five are from nearly four hundred awards, the rest virtually all the most prestigious universities in the United States and abroad. What to conclude? To me, then, the question was, with what to contend? I wasn't sure how outstanding my proposal was. I had nobody else from an outstanding institution to attest that it was outstanding. I didn't apply.

Should I have applied for these awards? Teaching at a second-rate university makes it especially difficult to know; you lack contacts to show that the miracle is possible, or to give some knowledge about how to negotiate the rules or master the requisite idioms. (A man I know at Princeton told me the other day that he should have initially contacted for his book the less prestigious publisher he wound up with, but "I was looking for a bigger kill." What breezy incisiveness! I thought. Nobody I work with talks this way, much less about such things. Sometimes it's just a matter of *talk*.) Furthermore, you risk sinking into self-pity when you resign yourself to giving up, while the very American discourse over anything to do with giving up assails you with every kind of uplift: think positive—there are just enough exceptions from unexceptional places who have gotten national awards, or gotten out, or gotten some wider, unexpected, unexplainable success. Theoretically, you are never precluded from being one of these. At worst, you know that you will never really know why you weren't one of the exceptions. Once I thought of submitting an article to a professional journal with a cover letter that had a letterhead from Michigan or Cornell. (I chanced to have copies of both.) I didn't. If I'd gotten the piece accepted, how could I be sure that my presumed affiliation had been a factor, any more than I could be sure, any single time, that my real affiliation had been a factor when I'd gotten rejected? Prestige is everywhere and nowhere. It explains everything and nothing to say that it seldom ceases to be "a factor."

I've taught in four countries outside the United States. No one appeared to be similarly baffled in any of them, certainly not in China, where universities such as Xiamen or Zhengzhou are so purely regional that they simply cannot be in any way compared to the premier institutions, Beijing University and Fudan. There is only one "rate." This is not merely because of the system of higher education in China, whereby Beijing and Fudan are larger, nationally competitive, and more generously funded. It would not occur to teachers at Xiamen or Zhengzhou to feel that where they are is second-rate because their "mission" is on a smaller, more localized, less culturally significant and internationally competitive scale than the premier universities.

The situation is not different in Brazil or Egypt. Nonetheless, I believe it is fair to say that a teacher at Maringa or Mansoura assumes a fundamentally different professional horizon than a counterpart either at the University of São Paulo or Campinas, or at Cairo University or the American University in Cairo. There is no interaction at all between what in America would be termed first- and second-rate universities, and, in order to understand how some sort of interaction gets founded in the first place, an American need look no further than athletics.

No country in the world has its system of higher education more thoroughly organized to enable athletic competition among its institutions than the United States. The effect this organization has, in turn, upon other kinds of competition, and the kinds of identity necessary to facilitate it, is incalculable. In 1990, for example, Robert Morris College played the University of Kansas (ranked No. 2 in the national polls) in the first round of the NCAA Division I basketball playoffs. There may have been no other basis for comparing the two institutions. Nevertheless, for a moment, there was a clear athletic occasion. My point is that the athletic structure cannot contain the competition within its own exclusive terms, and, indeed, the organization of some sports (wrestling, lacrosse, or women's basketball, especially) actually functions to challenge, by virtue of the competition itself, all other rationales whereby the privilege of the top universities is secure from the lesser ones.

One could argue that, whether in terms of its own peculiar athletic classification or some higher one, each American university has a chance to be No. 1. This potential is just as decisively American as the historical traditions that make it possible for our students to be so geographically mobile, or as the social ideals of individual effort that define how hard they work. Robert Morris didn't beat Kansas in the 1990 playoffs. But it came close. It could have. Zagazig, on the other hand, will never have a chance to come close to beating Cairo in anything, and therefore the terms that comprehend how the latter is incomparable to the former in everything are the more inflexible and complete.

Of course the sheer *decisiveness* of an athletic event—you either have the most numbers of some kind at the end or you don't—cannot be reproduced in a context such as the impeccably academic one I've been examining, whose essence is that it does not stage such "events" at all. (Very amusing to think of two finalists for a Woodrow Wilson going one-on-one.) In the academic world, where all universities are supposed to have "nice" reputations and where all departments are safely distant from the hindmost of their respective disciplines, the refusal to consider athletic correspondences may be a professional necessity. It's not the other way around, hence the joke at the University of Oklahoma about having a university to make the football team proud. Or the fancy a former colleague and I bred years ago about offering ourselves to Harvard on the basis either of a two-for-one trade (we'd each offer to teach a semester while doing janitorial work during the other one) or even a "player to be named later" (this last because we never figured out how Harvard could get somebody to come to Clarion). Correspondences between the athletic and the academic are distinctively American, however they are made, and they will not be abolished by being refused. Such correspondences are, I believe, crucial to our mythologies about class or our beliefs about how education equalizes because they express an antagonistic energy or fluid evaluative possibility that no other country has in higher education.

All the more curious, then, that the institutional setting of higher education academizes these energies in such rigid ways by sorting them out on a basis that in other countries would be comparable to class. Different universities can meet in athletic competition, but they do not compete discursively. For example, at the present moment the profession of English is engaged in a historicizing of itself, through a consideration of such questions as how literary studies originated, what role theory played, what role ideology, and so on. Once again, the universities I have taken to be in the position of the second-rate—not to say the very category of the second-rate—have played little part in the assessment; as Gerald Graff concedes at the outset in *Professing Literature*, "Most of my evidence is drawn from research-oriented departments of English at major universities."[2] I have already stated that one thing teaching at a second-rate university brings with it is the absence of any public discourse about the experience. It would be easy to claim that another thing such teaching provides is the continual spectacle of how one's own institution is lost to history.

If it exists as such a wholly derived thing, one could ask, of course, on what basis an institution such as Clarion merits some historical consideration? Don't the histories of the major universities, in other words, speak well enough for a Clarion? I'm not sure how to reply. Although the very history of Clarion is in no way unique—it has had its presidents, its deans for whom buildings are named, its conflicts over affirmative action, and even its one major-league pitcher—its agenda is not exactly that of major universities, and its nuances are not all explicable in terms either of those universities or of smaller, more exclusive liberal arts colleges. Subject as its English department is, to take one instance, to all the shifts of public policy about how important it may be to turn out secondary school teachers or to teach composition, there is a sense in which the department's myth of "shared humanistic values" (as Graff examines them) suits its recurrent need to defend itself as well as link its destiny to timeless pieties. And yet the campus has little of that note of pious, earnest, "Benton College" culture so vividly caught in the very first paragraph of Randall Jarrell's *Pictures from an Institution*, and it lacks such wonderfully corny details as the following from the fictional Waindell College of Nabokov's *Pnin*: "murals displaying recognizable members of the faculty in the act of passing on the torch of knowledge from Aristotle, Shakespeare, and Pasteur to a lot of monstrously built farm boys and girls."[3] I don't suppose Clarion is large enough, on the other hand, to absorb Nabokov's eccentric professor with the anonymity to which he is accustomed. Pnin, if he could exist on such a campus, would probably have had to profess concern, along with everybody else, when the football team was having a lousy season. Even to one who has taught at Clarion for a long time, its energies are so flat, so monotonous that the institution can seem, as someone explained a character in a contemporary novel, "so parodistically clear as to be unreadable."

That is, if anybody's reading, or reading anything more than departmental or administrative memos. I believe the point to make about a university such as Clarion is not so much why anybody outside should read it, or even what sort of text it affords, as that no one does.[4] It is not simply that what there is to read of a Clarion appears more fully and excitingly readable elsewhere. Second-rate universities, by definition, aren't newsworthy. Nor do they write or publish very much to read. If anyone at one does, the work is modeled on what first-rate schools produce or it won't get published.

One of the most revealing examples of this structural hierarchy I know is contained in the letters forum of a recent *PMLA*. Among those writing in reply to a column by Stanley Fish, in which he disputes the notion of "intrinsic merit" while arguing against *PMLA*'s longstanding policy of publishing only on the basis of blind submission, is a man from Southern Illinois University, Edwardsville. He maintains that in fact Fish wants "to extend tenure into the realm of publishing," for the politics of Fish's position are bent on "enhancing the power of those already far more powerful at the expense of those aspiring to join them." The revealing moment is this in Fish's reply: "And when Skoblow complains that I do not address the 'political needs of poor laborers' like himself, my response is, 'But that's *your* job, Jeffrey, since they're your needs.'"[5]

What are Fish's needs? How are they different from those of his critic? Of course Fish doesn't have to say. (He is most defensive about his original article when it is read as an account of his needs, for, so read, his take on the profession of course no more converts into all of it than Duke converts into SIU, Edwardsville.) It's as apparent that Fish's needs are different from Skoblow's as it is that his institution is different from his critic's. It's equally apparent that this difference is a hierarchical one, although the securely eminent Fish—who begins one of his most important essays with a quotation from a baseball player—treats his audience to the rare spectacle of this hierarchy being flaunted. After explicitly registering the difference in level between him and "Jeffrey," Fish goes on to note that because of him one of what he presumes are Jeffrey's needs has been met: Jeffrey has gotten published in "the profession's leading journal." A better demonstration of how SIU, Edwardsville is at best parasitic upon Duke can scarcely be imagined. And it falls only upon the "needs" of the professor at the second-rate institution to have to point this out, and to ponder the consequences.

In departments of English, if not in American higher education as a whole, professional self-consciousness has probably reached such a heightened state that it might now be possible to make a study of such moments as the one above, when institutional levels are marked, like badges or boundaries, during the course of an argument. My sense is that in print today these levels are seldom breached. Far more typical, I think, is another moment in the recent *Critical Inquiry* where the eminent feminist critics, Sandra Gilbert and Susan Gubar, dispute an equally eminent Frank Lentricchia by characterizing him as "no doubt a highly paid full professor at a prestigious private institution."[6] Here we have two full professors from, respectively, Princeton and Indiana, sneering at another from Duke. What if Lentricchia were not from Duke? Would they then have refrained from sneering? Or perhaps been more gentle and tried to avoid sounding patronizing if he were instead from Stockton State or Ball State, to take two universities from their respective states to which their own universities no doubt have a very different relation?

But not, however, a relation that would play in the pages of *Critical Inquiry*. Indeed, a Lentricchia from either of these second-rate universities I've just named is a Lentricchia hardly imaginable as a worthy opponent of Gilbert and Gubar. And suppose we switch this speculation from the point of view of producers to that of consumers. If one is not a reader from Princeton, Indiana, or Duke (besides the second of these, the other contributors to this particular issue of *Critical Inquiry* are from Rutgers, Hopkins, Brown, UC Santa Cruz, Cincinnati, and Chicago—a fair enough sample, with a possible exception, of first-rate institutions), why read the magazine? It is not, surely, to consolidate or advance one's own second-rate needs, which, as Fish discloses, only proceed on the basis of a first-rate model. There may be second-rate terms. There are undeniably second-rate journals. But such terms are barely, if at all, representable—unless, I think, one begins to recreate them as having to do with teaching. And if they have to do with teaching, although there might be some point to reading *Critical Inquiry*, there is less point in trying to get published there, and far less opportunity. People in second-rate schools, in my experience, teach four courses each semester (the man whom I earlier noted as having once taught seven was not teaching at a community college), which does not leave much time—especially if one is teaching English and half the load is composition—to read the newspaper, much less *Critical Inquiry*. *Critical Inquiry*, meanwhile, can be forgiven for not finding such a state of affairs particularly interesting—and either dismissing its consideration to other, more "practically" oriented magazines, or trying to refrain from lamenting the fateful resentment that all academic flesh is heir to, especially if a body doesn't have time to do enough research.

Ultimately teaching at a second-rate university is to acknowledge a ceaseless condition of structural exclusion from any decision about what can and cannot be authoritatively said. Of course there need to be qualifications. There are so many universities in the United States that breed so many differences among themselves as to make unlocatable the one difference I've been trying to find. Not all universities recognized as first-rate deserve the reputation. The large research universities may contain more sheer second-rateness (as if it were a material substance that could be quantified) than all the Clarions in the land, and even a Clarion is not entirely without either its incarnations of, or ambitions for, distinction.

In his magisterial study, *Distinction*, Pierre Bourdieu states: "The seemingly most formal oppositions within . . . social mythology always derive their ideological strength from the fact that they refer back, more or less discreetly, to the most fundamental oppositions within the social order: the opposition between the dominant and the dominated, which is inscribed in the division of labor, and the opposition, rooted in the division of the labor of domination, between two principles of domination, two powers, dominant and dominated."[7] This is a richly mediated claim and not completely suited to my purpose; as Fish points out to "Jeffrey," a host is not the same thing as a boss, and as I suggest in my discussion of *Critical Inquiry*, what Bourdieu would term "the division of the labor of domination" requires that there be readers as well as writers, and so therefore labor itself is situated to get quite vitally confused in terms of who owns what and even what is getting produced. Nonetheless, I take Bourdieu's framework to reemphasize my own focus: institutional affiliation is crucial to American higher education because it reproduces the opposition between first- and second-rate universities, which, in turn, represents the opposition between the dominant and the dominated.

The peculiar ideological formation by which this opposition is academically structured is one that maintains that "academic reputation" (there are many other phrases) can be common to both types of institution, and therefore there is actually no opposition between them. At most, opposition is transformed into levels or gradations. Bourdieu, on this point, has an especially nice assertion that while the fundamental opposition supports any number of lesser ones it is "euphemizing itself to the point of misrecognizability." The common discourse the dominated share with the dominant may not be entirely euphemistic in the mutuality of interest it presumes among levels of American higher education, but I believe this discourse does sustain misrecognitions everywhere. To speak of Clarion's academic reputation is to ignore or misrecognize much better reputations, as well as how these reputations exist to command both what an academy and a reputation are in the first place.[8]

And what are they? Ultimately a matter of privilege. Secondrate universities receive first-rate privilege as if it were a commodity and then simultaneously disseminate it as the institution's own or pass it further down—not only to high schools but to still more unrepresentable third- and fourth-rate universities. Privilege becomes indistinguishable from its function. The recognition of privilege is transformed, in turn, into privilege itself. During one year I was one of a group of teachers utterly absorbed in trying to understand the bizarre, sinister society of Saudi Arabia. Months passed. We felt that no one understood as much as we did. Then one night we met the visiting son of another teacher who had recently graduated from Oxford with a degree in Islamic studies. His disquisition on Muslim history and theology was brilliant. The smallest details of our daily life were revivified. We realized all over again that we were not scholars of the traditions informing this life. Our knowledge had no privilege. What I remember most is how my Australian colleague, who had long ago grown tired of being stereotyped by the British as a boozy lout, cursed the luminary who had so improbably appeared in our midst: "Those damn lads from Oxford. They're expected to be brilliant and they are. But you never know if they got brilliant just because they were expected to be." Is it always so with privilege? That night we were all moved to acknowledge Oxford rather than its graduate. Cursing it felt like another form of celebration. The dominated and the dominant: it may be the essence of this opposition as it plays itself out in academic terms that each half of the opposition comes to recognize its need for the other. I don't know about the view from Oxford, but that night I think we were all happy to have offered so much dim ignorance in order that Oxford could have a chance to shine.

I want to conclude with another, far more elaborate and

formal example of institutional recognition and how one version of the personal sinks while another gets promoted. A few years ago I was selected to serve on a nationwide panel assembled to choose applicants for government funding of projects that combined research and teaching. There were many guidelines. Institutional affiliation was not one. Indeed, since virtually all the candidates were from first-rate institutions (the one clear exception was quickly dismissed—even the typing quality of the proposal did not measure up to the rest) reputation should not have mattered very much at all, it seemed to me. Wrong. It was decisive at every turn. I came away from the day-long deliberations stunned that I could have assumed otherwise. Had my mostly second-rate experience of first-rate occasions left me to feel that somehow evaluative matters were different at the top? Had I presumed they were more balanced? More relaxed? Surely, at least, less sordid. One of my favorite lines had been for years one I read somewhere: "Academic politics is particularly vicious because the stakes are so low." Surely they wouldn't be so vicious if the stakes were higher. I'm not sure now if I should have known that at the top the viciousness—granted, the word here sounds too, well, *vulgar*—is just more refined, not to say, almost, refined away.

The two most prestigious institutions represented by my fellow panelists were, respectively, Yale and UCLA. It followed that both men spoke more than the rest of us, more authoritatively, and, in the case of the man from Yale, more eloquently. This man fascinated me. In such a setting I'd never witnessed such smooth, sophisticated judgment—the kind you hone through considerable experience at big tables, confident that all your energies are enjoying their proper scale. I didn't belong beside this man, any more than Clarion did beside Yale—and yet here we were anyway, only in America, and in a panel so artificially conceived that it could only have been the product of governmental decree. It took me a while to get over my self-consciousness at serving as a peer of someone from Yale for the first time in my life. (Me as the improbable Israeli to this man's still more improbable Auden.) It never occurred to me to wonder what the man from Yale might have thought; he appeared to handle some possible qualification to his position with perfect equanimity.

When we clashed, as I suppose we had to, it was brief, and, surely, memorable only to me. At one point I disputed something an applicant had claimed. Yale took me by the hand thus: "Suppose we look at it this way. You loan me some money. You have some reason to doubt that I'll pay you back. You may not completely trust me as a person. But if we consider *ethos* in the Aristotelian sense of the term . . ." I suppressed the impulse to snap: "You mean, we should trust this guy just because he's from Cornell?" I don't recall how I responded, only how I swooned inside as if with a revelation: ethos, yes, exactly, it was all a matter of ethos. We should trust this guy because he's from Cornell, a school fairly rank with ethos. Our choices, ultimately, had been dictated by assessments of relative ethos, which had to be so finely discriminated they usually wound up being crude. Meanwhile, where is it that Aristotle talks about ethos? Should I have leaned over and asked Yale for the reference? Maybe if you've really got ethos you don't actually have to read Aristotle.

Do you have ethos if you're from Bates College? If you compete against someone from Clarion you do. Bates, alas, was in another league on this occasion. My colleague from UCLA was not impressed at all when a man from Bates came up for consideration. Bates was all right, he allowed, but had no graduate school, and besides, this man from there was dull, dull; we were urged to ax him, especially those of us who didn't know him. I tried to resist. After all, for example, the man had more than one book. UCLA looked right at me and proceeded to give me at least as memorable a rejoinder as Yale: "Put it this way. All right, he's got books. But if he were any good would he still be at Bates?"

There we had it—a resoundingly self-evident question right out of the heart of *ethos*. I couldn't answer. I was speechless, silenced; of course everything rises that deserves to rise, because if it hasn't risen it hasn't deserved to. In the terms that I've been employing, what's first-rate is finally and fatefully separable from what's second-rate, or else it wouldn't be first-rate. For this great difference to be posited at all it must be at some crucial point completely and absolutely exclusive. Moreover, its value must be self-evident. The man from Bates with his books constituted an example of self-evidence divided against itself; if second-rateness can present first-rate credentials of some kind the very distinction may not be so obvious; worse, the very category of value is threatened as something conceivably arbitrary. This is why it is necessary to extricate the man from the institution; we may not know who he is (we may not want to know), but we know what Bates is.

Teaching at a second-rate university isn't to be deprived of ethos. It's to be deprived of integrity. Nothing—not the new computer center, not the semester's big drama production—is self-evidently itself. It abides instead in a continual inferiority; the nearest major university has far more computers and no one could expect that a small campus could stage something really good. Being second-rate is not a fraud—as long as one knows one's place, and keeps it. But, then, can there be something genuinely second-rate? The question is similar to that about whether there can be genuine kitsch, which usually receives the following answer: not if kitsch actually aspires to art; if kitsch and art weren't finally antithetical or oppositional terms, why is one speaking of kitsch at all? Similarly, if a second-rate university weren't finally in opposition to a first-rate one, why would it be necessary to make the basic distinction? A second-rate university continues at the definitional pleasure of a first-rate university, and, like kitsch, is probably better off being unaware that any sort of cultural domination is going on at all.

What is worth knowing? Teaching at a second-rate university is knowing, at least, that you're not worth knowing. A while ago at a conference I was talking to a friend who teaches at a university pretty much on Clarion's level. It was his first year there. Back in the United States after many years teaching in another country, he was lucky to get a job here at all. We were joined by an eminent scholar we both happened to know, who asked my friend where he was now. "Never heard of that one," responded the eminence, with a tone of such sweet, almost jaunty bemusement that for a moment I wished—what? That "that one" didn't even exist? (So few would ever hear of it.) No. That my own "one" didn't? No. (What the hell, it's a job, and there are worse places.) Perhaps I wished that there were merely a world where universities were more like towns, some, at least, so obscure that so much as to hear of their existence would prompt charm and wonderment. Certainly, as far as my friend and I were concerned, the prestige enjoyed by our man made him appear from another world. He's a decent man. Each time I see him, I feel as if we're both part of the same world. But we're not. Professionally, we move across a surface where only certain routes count, only certain places are comprehended as having depths, and only certain destinations can be found on the map.

NOTES

PREFACE

1. James Bennett, "The Essay in Recent Anthologies of Literary Criticism," *Substance* 17, no. 3 (1989): 107.

2. Linda Brodkey concludes her first chapter thus: "So to the extent that academics inherit a culture, but literally construct a practice out of the material resources of that culture, including the language in which to voice commitments to things academic, one might say that academics are what they read and write and publish." See Brodkey, *Academic Writing as a Social Practice* (Philadelphia: Temple University Press, 1987), 23. One indeed might. I might so offer this book. My "commitment," however, is just as much to what Brodkey keeps referring to as "lived experience" (in her later chapter on critiques of authority in ethnographic narratives) and how "things academic" unremittingly deform it. In this sense, I suppose, the following chapters are less about the social function of human subjectivity than about how it rather haplessly fails, at once insufficient and excessive for so many academic occasions. Whether my account finally enlarges the scene of writing or enriches the language available for academic experience I must leave my reader to judge. See also my comments on Watkins below.

3. Richard Ohmann, *English in America* (New York: Oxford University Press, 1976), 212.

4. Ed Cohen, "Are We (Not) What We Are Becoming? 'Gay Identity,' 'Gay Studies,' and the Disciplining of Knowledge," in Joseph Boone and Michael Cadden, eds., *Engendering Men* (New York: Routledge, 1990), 163–65.

5. Pierre Bourdieu, *Homo Academicus* (Palo Alto: Stanford University Press, 1988), 3.

6. Compare Greg Ulmer on "the anecdote inscribed in a theoretical text." The result, one might say, is a transformation of the ordinary rather than its confirmation. Ulmer writes the following of the conceptual provocations of the anecdote: "It is told not for its informational interest, not in reference to a prior life, but as part of a 'speculative' structure—the mise en abyme—a double take in which the narrative development of the event has formal, conceptual, explanatory consequences (it is the movement of the bobbin, away and back, that organizes Freud's formulation of the pleasure principle)." See Ulmer, *Teletheory* (New York: Routledge, 1989), 92. Of course it is always a question of what includes what. If the theoretical text has now been included in the academy, I think it is fair to say that the anecdote has not yet been included in the theoretical text—because the anecdotal continues to be excluded from discursive practices of the academy. The anecdotal flourishes in the discursive practices of journalism, on the other hand; Dinesh D'Souza's *Illiberal Education: The Politics of Race and Sex on Campus* (New York: Free Press, 1991) is, for example, full of anecdotes, as if to act out their effacement in academic discourse as he goes about constructing his own ideological narrative. A book such as D'Souza's uses anecdotes without any theoretical awareness, except perhaps to represent a strategy whereby some sort of "inside" experience is certified; D'Souza's acknowledgments only disclose how far his account is from such experience, as he thanks his two research assistants and numerous others for "valuable leads and suggestions."

7. Stanley Fish, *Doing What Comes Naturally* (Durham: Duke University Press, 1989), 386–87.

8. Evan Watkins, *Work Time: English Departments and the Circulation of Cultural Value* (Stanford: Stanford University Press, 1989), 21.

9. The passage continues as follows about utopian promise: "For work is then both a source of value 'in itself,' and the sign of an as yet unrealized moment when, the devises of manipulation exposed for what they are, work practices at last come into their own, freely available to anyone and everyone to exercise as they will." See Watkins, 159–60. But of course the whole point about a letter of application is that it would cease to function if it could be "freely available" for the individual will, even if there remains some good in "exposing" the "manipulation." What good? It's hard to say. As we read elsewhere: "If you work in a university, whatever you do or drain away from doing into some as yet uncolonized territory *will be put to use*" (Watkins, 164).

10. See James Clifford and George Marcus, *Writing Culture: The*

Poetics and Politics of Ethnography (Berkeley: University of California Press, 1986), 253.

11. Gayatri Spivak, "The New Historicism: Political Commitment and the Postmodern Critic," in H. Arum Veeser, ed., *The New Historicism* (New York: Routledge, 1988), 277.

12. Geoffrey Galt Harpham, "Constraints, not Consequences," *Times Literary Supplement*, 9–15 March 1990, 247.

13. Barbara Hernstein Smith, "Introduction," *Profession 89*, 3.

14. Paul Smith, *Discerning the Subject* (Minneapolis: University of Minnesota Press, 1988), xxxiv–xxxv.

15. Don DeLillo, *White Noise* (New York: Penguin, 1985), 11.

16. Daniel O'Hara has an intriguing reading of the subjective energies invested in such "transcendence" (my term). "The theorist," he states, concerning "the performance of a certain cultural ritual of postmodern intellectuals," "assembles from the collective archive figures, texts, contexts, issues, problems and questions and reconfigures them into a story told according to the constraints of professional conventions upon personal desire, as these constrain to apply . . . to the theorist in question." See O'Hara, "Selves in Flames: Derrida, Rorty, and the New Orthodoxy in Theory," *Contemporary Literature* 32, no. 1 (Winter 1991): 117. Of course some are more capable of such theoretical narratives than others; "A Derrida or Rorty has more freedom in this respect than a lesser known person," O'Hara parenthetically notes. See also John Michael's review of Fish, "Fish Shticks: Rhetorical Questions in Stanley Fish's *Doing What Comes Naturally*," *Diacritics* 20, no. 2 (Summer 1990): 54–74, on Fish's anxiety over being simultaneously masterful and embedded.

17. Watkins is of course not "free" enough (in O'Hara's sense) to be accorded the license to be playing with masks. No matter that he is, and in deeply engaging ways. Fish, on the other hand, is so free. Michael's review is especially good at, so to speak, finding Fish out, not so much through his rhetoric as after the rhetoric is over. Michael concludes: "Fish seems to play the anxious and distorting game with uncertainty that de Man finds others playing with theory, calling it a tiger in order to show that it is a paper tiger" (Michael, 73). About what is Fish so uncertain? Michael doesn't say, as if out of respect for, if not in tribute to, Fish's masks, although he does suggest one reason: "embeddedness itself—its totality, its inexorability" (see Michael, 66).

18. Richard Ohmann, *Politics of Letters* (Middletown: Wesleyan University Press, 1987), 271.

19. Roland Barthes, *The Grain of the Voice: Interviews 1962–80* (New York: Hill and Wang, 1985), 364.

20. Don DeLillo, *Libra* (New York: Viking, 1988), 108.

21. Theodore Ziolkowski, "The Ph.D. Squid," *American Scholar* (Spring 1990): 177–95.

22. Watkins's way of putting this is to further distance his own work from "what began long before in the schools as a systematic destruction of expectations." "It is," he continues, "the continual, palpable, tangible, intrusive presence of an enemy who seems to have been around every corner all your life" (Watkins, 276). I would position my own work differently, and, as I've stated, more skeptically. Let me suggest another way by citing an essay by Spivak in which at one point she notes how a Margaret Drabble text changes its narrative unity from third person to first. She goes on to dismiss the idea "that there is somewhere a way of speaking about truth in 'truthful' language, that a speaker can somewhere get rid of the structural unconscious and speak without role playing." She concludes as follows: "When one involves oneself in the microstructural moments of practice that make possible and undermine every macrostructural theory, one falls, as it were, into the deep waters of the first person who recognizes . . . the precarious necessity of the micro-macro opposition, yet is bound not to give up." See Spivak, "Feminism and Critical Theory," in Dan Latimer, ed., *Contemporary Critical Theory* (New York: Harcourt Brace Jovanovich, 1989), 653. I understand Paul Smith quoting Adorno to be marking the space where he gives up. I believe I begin, in contrast, within this same space because I don't want to give up. I'm implicated anyway in some more sovereign macrostructural practice of the Great Critic, just as Fish would have it. Of course the finer question is, how much of a macrostructural practice has to be registered in order to authenticate a microstructural one? Is merely to ask this question to fear that your own fateful "deep waters" are finally just so much shallow thrashing? Or, macrostructural awareness be damned, is to ask this question *already* to distance oneself too far from the suffering that might have prompted one to ask it in the first place?

23. Jane Tompkins, "Me and My Shadow," *New Literary History* 19, no. 1 (Autumn 1987): 169.

24. This essay can be compared to a later one where the "veiled language" of criticism conceals a violence comparable to that of a Western but is not a violence that needs to be genderized. See Tompkins, "Fighting Words: Unlearning to Write the Critical Essay," *Georgia Review* 42, no. 3 (Fall 1988): 585–90. Contrast Marianna Torgovnick, "Experimental Critical Writing," in *Profession 90*, who mentions neither violence nor gender, and whose call for "writing as a person with feelings, histories and desires" (27) seems to avoid more problems than it confronts.

25. Michel Foucault, *Power/Knowledge: Selected Interviews and Other Writings 1972–77* (New York: Random House, 1980), 94.

26. Charles Altieri, "When the Self Became the Subject: A Review Essay on Paul Smith," *Southern Humanities Review* 23, no. 3 (Summer 1989): 260.

CHAPTER ONE: *Absence in Letters of Recommendation*

1. John Carlos Rowe—in a rare recent discussion—considers letters of recommendation simply as among the " 'occasional writings' " of "our textual community," whereby we "sustain an ongoing conversation about our aims and purposes as intellectuals." See Rowe, "The Ethics of Professional Letters: Eleven Theses," *Profession 90*, 48. Thus an institutional relation is exchanged for a more personal one, and a series of rhetorical guidelines is presented under the auspices of something ethical. Rowe never questions letters of recommendation; his presumption of them as constituting a "conversation" gives him no basis for doing so. (Hence he is content to argue that computers should do more of the talking, except about candidates for tenured positions, who already have enough said through teaching evaluations and publications.) My own view of them as texts could not be more contrary. For example, there is Wayne Booth's brief mention of how, one day, faced with the task of writing an overdue letter of recommendation, he has to stop at one point to read a bit of his former student's dissertation so that he won't appear in the letter to be like the many others about whom Booth has composed recommendations. See Booth, *The Vocation of a Teacher* (Chicago: University of Chicago Press, 1988), 248–49. Earlier in his "journal," Booth ruminates that if to his eight million words of comments on short papers were added "the half million or so churned into letters of recommendation, I begin to rival the great letter-writers like Voltaire—in quantity. Of course, if you then divide by the number of repetitions—of catchwords, of 'encouraging phrases,' of expressions of alarm—the total number shoots down by 573 percent" (Booth, 239).

2. John Gross, *The Rise and Fall of the Man of Letters* (New York: Collier Books, 1970), 159. Gosse got the post.

3. Howard Gardner, *Art, Mind, and Brain: A Cognitive Approach to Creativity* (New York: Basic Books, 1982), 361–62.

4. That these same Blakes, in their pedagogical guise, deal with students by recreating their texts for study in terms of their radicalizing potential reveals, I think, how thorough and finally unproblematic is the romance of selfhood in the profession. Richard Ohmann, for example, a fierce critic of the profession, nevertheless gives as his own pretty much the standard ideology of any introductory literature course: "Every good poem, play, or novel is revolutionary, in

that it strikes through well grooved habits of seeing and understanding." See Ohmann, *English in America* (New York: Oxford University Press, 1976), 46. For a critique of this ideology, see Evan Watkins, *Work Time: English Departments and the Circulation of Cultural Value* (Stanford: Stanford University Press, 1989), perhaps beginning with his distinction "between how work in English often appears an organization designed somewhere else and imposed on those who do it, and at the same time an organization generated by those *in* English and imposed on others" (88). The compensatory emphasis on selfhood, we could say, arises because the discipline is "designed" somewhere else, where the claims of "system" are far more important.

5. But what *is* force? A mere word? Or is the profession resigned to it (if less happily and self-consciously) very much as Stanley Fish is at the end of his reply to Gerald Graff regarding the essay, "Anti-Professionalism"? There Fish makes force coterminous with a triumphant rationality "whose force has become so great that it seems to be independent. Of course it is not independent, but it does occupy the *position* of independence in a system that is anchored by nothing more or less than the power it has achieved and continues to exercise." See Fish, "Resistance and Independence: A Reply to Gerald Graff," *New Literary History* 17, no. 1 (Autumn 1985): 126. ("Anti-Professionalism," along with a later essay, "Force," is reprinted in Fish, *Doing What Comes Naturally* [Durham: Duke University Press, 1989].) Fish on force is neither as supple nor as nuanced as Derrida on *différance*. At the end of his reply, Fish slyly uses the word again, or rather, he winks, uses it *as* a word, "a word I use without apology." Would force used as a word *with* apology be a quite different thing? Graff apparently thinks so, since his response to Fish renames Fish's villain as, in fact, "anybody who feels threatened by the reduction of interpretive authority to the question of which groups possess the power to force their standards on others." See Graff, "Interpretation on Tlön: A Response to Stanley Fish," *New Literary History* 17, no. 1 (Autumn 1985): 115. The apology, that is, would at last utter the true political character of a force that heretofore dare not speak its own name: Duke. See my comment in my last chapter on another Fish reply to someone who *is* "threatened." "Duke" is but another name for what I have referred to here as a disciplinary formation.

6. "Anti-professionalism is the very content of the profession itself," states Fish—rather notoriously and contentiously, I think—and then again: "Anti-professionalism is the very center of the professional ethos, constituting by the very vigor of its opposition the true form of that which it opposes." See Fish, "Anti-Professionalism," *New Literary History* 17, no. 1 (Autumn 1985): 99, 107. Any more than Fish, I don't see how venal motives and crass objectives can be understood

as such apart from a professional context that sets them over against aspiring reasons and significant purposes. But what about perfectly respectable motives that only had to do with teaching objectives? How would such a person represent the profession? He or she scarcely exists in the text of Fish, for whom elite standards are so fundamental that a mere teacher could almost be deemed not so much anti- as nonprofessional. Moreover, it is of course hard enough for the text of recommendation just to comprehend a subject who only teaches.

7. Magall Sarfatti Larson, *The Rise of Professionalism* (Berkeley: University of California Press, 1977), 227.

8. Cyril Connolly, *The Unquiet Grave* (1945; New York: Viking, 1966), 1.

9. Ralph Ellison, *Invisible Man* (1952; New York, 1982), 190–91.

10. Again, see Rowe, "Ethics," above. James Malek provides an even better instance of my contention because he denounces not merely "reference-letter inflation" (a familiar enough complaint, not to say the only one) but the authors. "What surprises me about these and many other letters," he writes, "is that they were written by people who spend a lot of time analyzing texts and thinking about writers and readers of texts. Perhaps referees need to be reminded that their letters do not simply disappear into a void—they are read by real human beings." See Malek, "Caveat Emptor: Or, How Not to Get Hired at DePaul," *ADE Bulletin* 92 (Spring 1989): 36. As always with letters of recommendation, somebody has to be "real," and it falls upon the reader to be so because both the authors and their subjects are, respectively, absent, creating the need to ground the enterprise in *some* reality. The problem with Malek's complaint is that he ignores the enterprise *is* an enterprise, embedded in institutional imperatives he elsewhere protests against, but only in their number rather than their nature. These imperatives are as "real" as the human beings whom they subject. Malek himself is undoubtedly one of these, although he presumes that he can miraculously intervene in order to insist that his presence, or that of any one reader's, can somehow right the entire issue. Alas, Malek is just another man who studies texts in order to be ensnared by them, as well as a chair who understandably prefers to hire people rather than supplements.

CHAPTER TWO: *Whom to Acknowledge?*

1. Stanley Cavell, *The Claim of Reason: Wittgenstein, Skepticism, Morality, and Tragedy* (New York: Oxford University Press, 1982), xxi–xxii. I cite these pages because they conclude a lengthy foreword.

2. One of the problems with Evan Watkins's otherwise comprehen-

sive treatment of academic work is that he neglects to consider its institutional site with his customary political sophistication. "As an abstract labor form," he writes, for example, "work in English involves multiple activities engaged in by a number of people concentrated at the same workplace" (see Watkins, *Work Time: English Departments and the Circulation of Cultural Values* [Stanford: Stanford University Press, 1989], 85). True enough. But this workplace is part of an institution, and many of these activities are shaped in quite peculiar ways by the sort of institution any one is and the kind of status it enjoys in terms of others. What I mean in this context is that faculty at first-rate institutions are simply expected to produce books and that their institutions are accordingly situated in terms of others of their class so that eminent lecturers can be invited, special workshops be held, and so on—all that is required to keep research energies stimulated as well as social contacts kept up.

3. S. P. Mohanty, "Us and Them: On the Philosophical Bases of Political Criticism," *Yale Journal of Criticism* 2, no. 2 (1989): 26.

4. Again, Stanley Cavell can be cited as composing a far more elegant as well as sincere turn on this *topoi* of acknowledging: thanking students. I am thinking especially of the moment in *Pursuits of Happiness* when he cautions that specific suggestions from films have not only come from friends, and then continues: "They can have come from a large class in which a student whose name I may not have learned asked a question I am not likely to forget." See Cavell, *Pursuits of Happiness: The Hollywood Comedy of Remarriage* (Cambridge: Harvard University Press, 1981), 277. Later, Cavell has the following amplification: "One of the best gratifications, and confirmations, in this work of reading is that discussion, well prompted, allows those who take an interest to make clear and notable contributions to it. This bears the promise of a communal enterprise" (278). In Cavell's acknowledgments the promise that so many others merely presume actually seems to have been made good because it feels so clearly good for Cavell to make acknowledgment of the promise.

5. Marianne Hirsch, *The Mother/Daughter Plot* (Bloomington: Indiana University Press, 1989), 22.

6. Paul Theroux, *World's End and Other Stories* (Boston: Houghton Mifflin, 1980), 210.

7. Michel Foucault, *Politics, Philosophy, Culture: Interviews and Other Writings 1977–1984*, ed. Lawrence D. Kritzman (New York: Routledge, 1988), 327.

CHAPTER THREE: *Lack of Application*

1. John Dos Passos, *U.S.A.* (1930; New York: Modern Library, 1937), 22.

2. Stanley Fish, "No Bias, No Merit: The Case Against Blind Submission," *PMLA* 103, no. 5 (October 1988): 745. This article appears as a chapter in Fish, *Doing What Comes Naturally* (Durham: Duke University Press, 1989).

3. Robert Walser, *Selected Stories* (New York: Farrar, Straus, Giroux, 1982), 26.

4. Edward Said, *Beginnings: Intention and Method* (New York: Basic Books, 1975), 36.

5. Once again, I must refer to my comments in the last chapter after citing Fish's reply to a "Jeffrey," who has objected to his effacement in what Fish terms "the political needs of poor laborers." A better disclosure of the power of what might be characterized as the major over the minor leagues could scarcely be imagined. Another reason I want to mark this moment in Fish at this point is because Fish himself is so given to athletic analogies. See John Michael's review of *Doing*, "Fish Shticks: Rhetorical Questions in Stanley Fish's *Doing What Comes Naturally*," *Diacritics* 20, no. 2 (Summer 1990): 54–74, especially 60–64, for the significance of such analogies.

6. Kenneth Burke, *Counter-Statement* (1930; Chicago: Phoenix Books, 1957), 126.

7. Lionel Trilling, "Of This Time, Of That Place," in Herbert Gold and David Stevenson, eds., *Stories of Modern America* (New York: St. Martin's, 1961), 81.

8. John Berryman, "Interview," in George Plimpton, ed., *The Paris Review Interviews: Writers at Work*, 4th series (London: Secker and Warburg, 1977), 306.

9. Alan Feldman, "Plea," *College English* 39, no. 8 (April 1978): 945.

10. James Joyce, *Ulysses* (New York: Random House, 1961), 636.

CHAPTER FOUR: *Croaking About Comp*

1. Cynthia Ozick, "The College Freshman: Portrait of a Hero as a Collection of Old Saws," *Confrontations* 33/34 (Fall/Winter 1986–87): 230.

2. Of course I don't know everyone who does. (And those I do know tend to share my views.) Just because I don't, and just because everyone doesn't hate comp as much as I do, doesn't mean that my own experience has no representative status. Much of my quarrel is with a

hegemonic representation so powerful in composition discourse that it can dismiss counter instances as not so much misrepresentations as trivializations, and there's the end of it. A reader for *College Composition and Communication* commented on an earlier, shorter draft of this chapter as follows: "I think we haven't written about teaching comp in the way that you would like us to because we all know too well what it can be like. We don't need to write about it. Reading fourteen pages of someone else's anger about it doesn't help me much—I still have to go out and do it."

3. Dana Heller, "Silencing the Soundtrack: An Alternative to Marginal Comments," *College Composition and Communication* 40, no. 2 (May 1989): 212.

4. William Gass, "Interview," in George Plimpton, ed., *Paris Review Interviews: Writers at Work*, 5th series (New York: Penguin, 1981), 279.

5. Donald M. Murray, "The Listening Eye: Reflections of the Writing Conference," in Richard Graves, ed., *Rhetoric and Composition: A Sourcebook for Teachers and Writers* (Upper Montclair, N.J.: Boynton/Cook, 1984), 263.

6. Michael Carter, "The Idea of Expertise: An Exploration of Cognitive and Social Dimensions of Writing," *College Composition and Communication* 41, no. 3 (October 1990): 265.

7. This being's existence is as everywhere present in composition theory as she or he is everywhere absent in literary theory. Consequently, it is especially interesting to see how The Student is situated in comp theory that has been influenced by, or participates in, poststructuralist literary theory. Edward Lotto, for example, concludes a highly sophisticated consideration of textuality thus: "But the most subtle obstacle in teaching our students is our own training in English departments, which are split between the demands of utterance and those of text." See Lotto, "Utterance and Text in Freshman English," *College English* 51, no. 7 (November 1989): 684. The venerable deconstructive opposition, in other words, is played out, once again, this time over the privileged ground of the student body. This body is not itself questioned. No freshman is discriminated against as an aporia. The student stands as transcendentally signified as if Lotto has never read Derrida or Fish.

8. John L'Heureux, *An Honorable Profession* (New York, 1990), 151. Compare the narrator of a story by Richard Burgin: "I start thinking about how I'd be better off in my apartment preparing for classes, except that by now I can teach these freshman English classes in my sleep." See Burgin, *Man Without Memory* (Urbana, 1989), 35. He doesn't say these are comp classes. I don't think he has to. Outside of the professional discourse, it is widely accepted, I believe, that comp

teachers are poor, overworked, undervalued souls. It is left to fiction to register this perception. Has an article entitled, "The Image of the Composition Teacher in Contemporary American Fiction," already been written?

9. Joseph Conrad, *Heart of Darkness*, 3d ed., ed. Robert Kimbrough (New York: W.W. Norton, 1988), 50. Lest my citation of *Heart of Darkness* seem too frivolous, compare Mary Rose O'Reilley's use of the same text in the same context. "Indeed," she writes, "the Heart of Darkness strikes me as an appropriate metaphor for the classroom in more ways than one. It's here we confront chaos and misrule, savage silence, chills, fever, and, at least in some places where I've taught, failure of the air-conditioning." See O'Reilley, "'Exterminate . . . the Brutes'—And Other Things That Go Wrong in Student-Centered Teaching," *College English* 51, no. 2 (February 1989): 142. Soon, however, O'Reilley is affirming the very pieties she began by doubting, distancing herself from her darkest sources by quoting others (whom she then compares to herself losing control over her children in the kitchen), and concluding in the following manner: "I'm happy to be in a profession that deals with life's basic issues. The question may not be, has this new pedagogy changed students, but has it changed us?" (O'Reilley, 146). This final move is once again typical of comp theory discourse when it confronts the fact that students either fail or change or don't appear to be able to do much of anything very dramatic. At least we can change, or ought to.

10. How much of the teaching of composition in American higher education is done by people who couldn't get jobs at institutions that do not require them to do it? (As Booth remarks, "many" people distinguish good jobs from bad on the basis of whether you have to teach composition [Booth, *Vocation*, 265].) Why couldn't they? See particularly my chapter on writing dissertations. Where are they instead? See my last on teaching at second-rate universities.

11. Vladamir Nabokov, *Strong Opinions* (New York: McGraw-Hill, 1973), 22.

12. Stanley Fish, *Doing What Comes Naturally* (Durham: Duke University Press, 1989), 354.

13. Robert Scholes, *Textual Power* (New Haven: Yale University Press, 1985), 85.

14. Another, less unlovely version of the same trope: "A man in the home office tends to conduct his business on the basis of the papers that come before him. After twenty-five years or more of that sort of thing, he finds it difficult sometimes to distinguish himself from the papers he handles and comes almost to believe that he and the papers constitute a single creature, consisting principally of hands

and eyes: lots of hands and eyes." From the notebooks of Wallace Stevens, as quoted by Helen Vendler, "Posthumous Work and Beautiful Subjects," *New Yorker* 66, no. 39 (12 November 1990): 132.

15. Howard Tinberg, " 'An Enlargement of Observation': More on Theory Building in the Composition Classroom," *College Composition and Communication* 42, no. 1 (February 1991): 38.

16. Quoted in Miriam DeCosta Willis, "Folklore and the Creative Artist: Lydia Cabrera and Zora Neale Hurston," *CLA Journal* 27 (September 1983): 86.

CHAPTER FIVE: *Drifting Through the MLA*

1. I think Wayne Booth's comment fairly represents a normative view of the organization: "The Modern Language Association remains a monstrous, largely unintelligible growth. It serves, and has almost always served, many ends, some in obvious conflict with others. It leads a swarming, cacophonous life that nobody could ever want to defend lock, stock, and barrel. And yet all of us here have decided to continue in uneasy support of this monster, even while pursuing our more sharply defined goals in other, smaller organizations." See Booth, *The Vocation of a Teacher* (Chicago: University of Chicago Press, 1988), 13. He is speaking in 1982 as the outgoing president. One curious feature of this characterization is that the monster threatens, apparently, only those inside it; nobody else, as several of Booth's other essays make sadly clear, pays much attention to it.

2. David Lodge, *Small World* (New York: Macmillan, 1984), 314.

3. Michel Foucault, *Discipline and Punish: The Birth of the Prison* (New York: Vintage, 1979), 165.

4. Roland Barthes, *The Pleasure of the Text* (New York: Hill and Wang, 1975), 18–19.

5. This might be a space for an especially fine Fishian point. Arguing against the view that instability or complexity of belief means that constraint is not in place, Fish emphasizes instead that "the fact that there is nothing monolithic about constraint . . . does not mean that [it] can be thought of as more or less loose, as possibly 'leaking' and opening up at the seams or at points of pressure where the possibility of actions or thoughts *not* constrained is waiting to be seized." Nuance all one wants to, he continues: "the nuances will never add up to a moment or a place where consciousness becomes transparent to itself and can at last act freely" (Stanley Fish, *Doing What Comes Naturally* [Durham: Duke University Press, 1989], 32). One way a discipline prevents nomads, in other words (such prevention providing an intriguing way to understand Fish's prominence), is by insisting that

nomadic behavior is a conceptual scandal because it *flaunts* constraint. Fish, incidentally, does not mention the MLA, although he does mention the presumably less "monstrous" examples of both the Spenser and the Milton societies. I fear I would only drift too far away here if I tried to take up in Fish's terms the question of how the number of conferences has proliferated in recent years—as if, in my own terms, an admittedly decentered discipline nonetheless acts to fix nomadic behavior by promoting it as professional.

    6. Cited in Jan Morris, ed., *The Oxford Book of Oxford* (New York: Oxford University Press, 1978), 369.

    7. Dean MacCannell, *The Tourist: A New Theory of the Leisure Class* (New York: Schoken, 1976), 13.

    8. Could one say, furthermore, that every convention within the profession of English that is not the MLA stages itself within the recognition that it is not? There is good reason, to take one example, for Cary Nelson, in an unusually frank discussion of conferences, to sense that the 1990 conference on "Crossing the Disciplines: Cultural Studies in the 1990s" at the University of Oklahoma might well have been called, "The 1980s: an MLA reunion." See Nelson, "Always Already Cultural Studies: Two Conferences and a Manifesto," in *Journal of the Midwest Modern Language Association* 24, no. 1 (Spring 1991): 27. Nelson, in passing, touches on some reasons why conferences have proliferated—so that graduate students and young faculty members can put a paper on a vita (despite tiny audiences at multiple-session time slots or, at Oklahoma, a $95 registration fee) or so that a university can present itself as a cutting-edge site, for little more than the cost of honoraria for a few keynote stars. He even draws a distinction between those conferences where everyone who answers an open invitation to submit papers is put on the program and those where either there is no such invitation (all papers are the result of invitation) or where inclusion on the program is the result of competition. This last category is the most compelling one, and the basic reason the MLA continues to abide as the transcendental signified of conferences is probably because it features the competitive edge necessary to produce the best papers. Whether in fact the competition to get a paper accepted for an MLA session is as open as advertised is another, and far more dubious, matter. It would take a separate paper to examine it. My sense, however, is that the more closed (that is, foreclosed) MLA sessions are, the more open all sessions at virtually all other conferences become—until we are fast approaching the moment when almost any paper submitted to any other conference somehow gets onto the program.

    9. Jacques Derrida, "Sending: On Representation," *Social Research* 49, no. 2 (Summer 1982): 310.

10. Ulmer, *Teletheory* (New York: Routledge, 1989), 92. One especially rich example is provided by his citation of Barthes on the essay, as an example of "the possibility of an argument or of a story without enigma": "The question itself keeps the mind pressing against a blank wall, thereby preventing it from ever finding an outlet. To show a man how to get out you first have to free him from the misleading influence of the question" (Ulmer, 109). The disciplinary narrative of constraint, of course, insists, on the contrary, that there is always a way out, because there is always the question, which is never misleading.

11. Walter Stone, "The Mezzanine," in William Phillips and Philip Rahv, eds., *The Partisan Review Anthology* (New York: Holt, Rinehart and Winston, 1962), 485.

CHAPTER SIX: *Being a White Male*

1. Hirsch, *The Mother/Daughter Plot* (Bloomington: Indiana University Press, 1989), 17.

2. Cohen, "Are We (Not) What We Are Becoming? 'Gay Identity,' 'Gay Studies,' and the Disciplining of Knowledge," in Joseph Boone and Michael Cadden, eds., *Engendering Men* (New York: Routledge, 1990), 161. One striking contrast to Hirsch is consequent upon an important distinction Cohen goes on to make: "The more I think about it, the more I realize that my 'identity crisis' is not so much a crisis about 'my identity' but rather my crisis with identity *per se*" (Cohen, 173). There is a difference between celebrating one's identity as plural and questioning whether or not an identity finally exists because of its capacity to be pluralized. It is tempting to make this difference, in turn, the measure of the basic one between feminists and gays. Cohen mentions that in graduate school he was a member of "an ad hoc group of 'fem-men-ists'" who were united under the motto 'we fuck with categories'" (Cohen, 174–75). Gays, we may say, are enabled by more categorical transgressions—including, as the very title of Cohen's group reveals, the category of feminism. Compare, for example, Helen Cixous: "A woman is never far from 'mother.' (I mean outside her role functions: the 'mother' as nonname and as source of goods.) There is always within her at least a little of that good mother's milk. She writes in white ink." See Cixous, "The Laugh of the Medusa," in Elaine Marks and Isabelle de Courtivron, eds., *New French Feminisms* (New York: Schocken, 1980), 251. There is simply nothing in the fact of being gay as comparably "essentialist," and therefore troubling, as the fact of motherhood is to being a feminist.

3. Alice Jardine and Paul Smith, eds., *Men in Feminism* (New York: Methuen, 1987), 88.

4. Joseph A. Boone and Michael Cadden, eds., *Engendering Men: The Question of Male Feminist Criticism* (New York: Routledge, 1990), 23–24.

5. In an extremely acute contribution to *Engendering Men*, Lee Edelman provides a reading of the Gilbert-Gubar controversy with Lentricchia that converges at several points with my own reading, below. One reason that Edelman is so acute is because he aims to confront directly the place of homosexuality in patriarchy, initially by criticizing Lentricchia for presuming that patriarchs can have access to "the unconscious of patriarchy itself—an unconscious that may be viewed as 'feminized' but must not be construed as female." See Edelman, "Redeeming the Phallus: Wallace Stevens, Frank Lentricchia, and the Politics of (Hetero)sexuality," in Boone and Cadden, *Engendering*, 40. Edelman's point is that if the patriarchal unconscious is seen instead as female it will be far more difficult to appropriate or domesticate it as "fundamentally other." What one wants to know, however, is the role of homosexuality in this unconscious. Although Edelman would presumably defer, as many do in his volume, to Eve Kosofsky Sedgwick's paradigm of how male rivals bond "homosocially" in order to maintain and transmit patriarchal power, he appears to exempt homosexuality from its "libidinal economy" on the basis of its being "other," without, however, clarifying how this otherness can then participate in the energies of the *homo*sexual, which would seem to be inescapably those of the *same*. Another way of speculating upon the future of male feminist criticism would be to wonder how far gay male critics will feel the need to distance themselves from those who aren't gay; what gay males gain in nonpatriarchal "otherness" they risk losing by being absorbed into the more comprehensive Otherness of feminists. Edelman seems to me to fudge this danger by characterizing homosexuality as something "which . . . may never be entirely assimilable" to feminism "but from which it is never wholly separable either" (Edelman, 45).

6. Frank Lentricchia, "Andiamo!" *Critical Inquiry* 14, no. 2 (Winter 1988): 412.

7. Sandra M. Gilbert and Susan Gubar, "The Man on the Dump Versus the United Dames of America; or, What Does Frank Lentricchia Want?" *Critical Inquiry* 14, no. 2 (Winter 1988): 404.

8. The gay contestation of the presumed heterosexuality of maleness is, precisely, the source of its own power. As Boone writes in *Engendering Men*, with reference to *Men in Feminism*, "Too many of the generalizations made about men's desire to become a part of feminism *take for granted* the 'heterosexual' basis of that desire" (Boone and Cadden, 23). Boone does not appear to write as a gay man. Nonetheless, it is by virtue of the force of the homosexual intervention that

he can ask such questions as the following: "How do we sometimes take advantage of our born status as 'men' to negotiate the treacherous process of establishing a professional identity and continuing to exist within the limitations of our specific institutional circumstances?" (Boone and Cadden, 24). Cohen, cited earlier from the same volume, would have a very pointed, energetic reply to such a question. A feminist would presumably have a quite different reply, especially if she felt it made no difference that, not finally unlike the proudly heterosexual Lentricchia, Boone was just using a freshly gendered context in order to pose the same old patriarchal question.

9. Deborah McDowell, "New Directions for Black Feminist Criticism," in Elaine Showalter, ed., *The New Feminist Criticism* (New York: Pantheon, 1985), 186. This is in 1980. Six years later Sandra O'Neale is making the same complaint: "I find it improbable to discuss the development of black women writers and characters in the language of American feminism. . . . the black woman has never been the feminine ideal, not only in the minds of men who write literature, but, more important, she has not been the ideal of femininity through which white women obtain their self-view; not even, lamentably, has she been an ideal for many black women." See O'Neale, "Inhibiting Midwives, Usurping Creators: The Struggling Emergence of Black Women in American Fiction," in Teresa de Lauretis, ed., *Feminist Studies/Critical Studies* (Bloomington: Indiana University Press, 1986), 143. One could cite many more versions of this same complaint. O'Neale's essay reveals, as do many others, that, notwithstanding her exclusion or deformation, she simply has no other language than that of American feminism in which to so much as pose the problem.

10. Barbara Johnson, *The Critical Difference* (Baltimore: Johns Hopkins University Press, 1985), x–xi.

11. George Orwell, *The Road to Wigan Pier* (1937: New York: Harcourt, Brace & World, 1958), 174–75.

12. Werner Sollors, ed., *The Invention of Ethnicity* (New York: Oxford University Press, 1989), x.

13. Henry Louis Gates, "The Master's Pieces: On Canon Formation and the African-American Tradition," *South Atlantic Quarterly* 89, no. 1 (Winter 1990): 105.

14. Henry Louis Gates, *Figures in Black: Words, Signs, and the 'Racial' Self* (New York: Oxford University Press, 1987), xxiii–xxiv.

15. Eve Kosofsky Sedgwick, "Across Gender, Across Sexuality: Willa Cather and Others," *South Atlantic Quarterly* 88, no. 1 (Winter 1989): 140.

16. In fact she writes this as an aside. Boone quotes it in *Engendering Men* ("to quote Jardine quoting Helene Cixous") as "one of the logical, crucial, and, I hope, inevitable directions in which an enlight-

ened discourse of masculinity will develop" (Boone and Cadden, 24). That he never pauses at least to consider how, theoretically anyway, a few men might experience some resentment about having the terms of their own "enlightenment" set so authoritatively by a woman is still another indication of how completely feminized are the available terms of some future masculine discourse. If it must be feminized, must it be completely so? Cannot some male discourse avail itself of female insights into how one sex transforms the other if it alone authorizes the questions? From Boone's example, anyway, the answer to these questions seems to be, first, yes, and, second, no.

17. One of the most interesting articles in *Engendering Men*, by Robert K. Martin, concludes thus: "The construction of male heterosexual identity, in response to a newly independent woman and to the emergence, for the first time, of homosexual identity in the mid-nineteenth century, meant the increased sequestration and limitation of women and rendered suspect all earlier forms of male intimacy." See Martin, "Hester Prynne, *C'est Moi*: Nathaniel Hawthorne and the Anxieties of Gender," in Boone and Cadden, 138. Martin's is a good example of what a male criticism might look like that does not have to advertise its feminism in order to be progressive as well as sophisticated. Note also the next essay by Mark Seltzer, who remarks rather testily in his notes that his paper "is not, by the way, about 'the question of male feminist criticism.' " See Seltzer, "The Love-Master," in Boone and Cadden, 306. I hope I have made clear how the question of why a man would want to say such a thing is possibly the one crucially unposed—perhaps unperceived—question in the volume.

18. Shoshana Felman, "Women and Madness: The Critical Phallacy," *Diacritics* 5 (Winter 1975): 10.

CHAPTER SEVEN: *On Not Writing a Dissertation*

1. This was the case, for example, with the man who is the Subject (his word) of William James's famous consideration, "The Ph.D. Octopus," published in 1903. The Subject's institution decrees that his appointment will be revoked unless he gets a Ph.D. from Harvard. The man writes a dissertation. It cannot be passed. "Brilliancy and originality by themselves won't save a thesis for the doctorate; it must also exhibit a heavy technical apparatus of learning, and this our candidate had neglected to bring to bear." Subsequently James's Subject wrote something adequate, passed his examination, "and brought his college into proper relations with the world again." See James, "The Ph.D. Octopus," in *Writings 1902–1910* (New York: Library of Congress, 1987), 1112. These "relations" are the ideology, which man-

dates, in part, that a man who teaches at a university "represent" it to the world, and represents it best by having demonstrated that he has been the dissertated "creature" of another university. It's very difficult to say how sarcastic James is in writing about these "relations." It's easier to be sarcastic—almost as a way of being more resigned—at century's end. See Theodore Ziolkowski's very different use of James in "The Ph.D. Squid," *American Scholar* (Spring 1990): 177–95.

2. B. L. Reid, *First Acts* (Athens: University of Georgia Press, 1987), 237, 238.

3. A research project very much worth pursuing: the number of Ph.D. candidates who get to the dissertation-writing stage, but never write one. Another project: the number of candidates who try to write a dissertation, but fail to get it accepted. Either project might be impossible to complete, and both represent, to me, how so little, beyond the achieved or accepted fact of dissertations, is actually known about them. And to consider a question whose data is somewhat more available for investigation: has anyone in any field not thanked his or her adviser or attempted some sort of disacknowledgment?

4. Consider the quite hilarious bit of scatology David Lavery quotes from the conclusion of a friend's dissertation. Of course it exists as written, yet, since it was accepted, as he says, one can only wonder if what the friend wrote was in fact read by the committee. See Lavery, "Dissertations as Fiction," *College English* 41, no. 6 (February 1980): 75–79. There must exist in the library stacks of Ph.D.-granting institutions all over the country similar examples from all disciplines of essentially unwritable antipathies that candidates have nevertheless managed to get into dissertations. Levery, unfortunately, does not go into this. His article mentions along the way the dissertation-smeared texts of Kurt Vonnegut Jr., Carlos Castenada, and Robert Pirsig toward a destination that calls for the time when dissertations will be accepted as fictions, having acknowledged the "fictional" (Nietzsche and Wallace Stevens are quoted) in themselves. Lavery still has one of the few searching accounts of what goes into the making of a dissertation that I've ever come across.

5. Here, in addition, let me acknowledge Stanley Fish in his chapter on "Force" in *Doing What Comes Naturally* (Durham: Duke University Press, 1989). Contemplating the fact in a legal context, Fish writes, for example: "The absence of external or independent constraints only means that the constraints inherent in the condition of belief—the condition of having been persuaded to some vision, the condition of not seeking but already occupying a position—are always and inescapably *in force*" (Fish, 522). In one very profound sense, my own experience of not writing a dissertation can be read as both a ratification of and as a dissent from Fish's argument. Some of the dis-

sent is from the "always." The rest lies in the "inescapably." See also the Fishy depths in my final chapter, where I go against the current more forcibly.

6. Roland Barthes, *S/Z* (New York: Hill and Wang, 1974), 45.

CHAPTER EIGHT: *On Teaching at a Second-Rate University*

1. Unaffected, that is, unless they happen to meet. Then there is going to be some displeasure. See, for example, the moment in Alice Munro's story, "Mischief," when Rose meets Jocelyn, who comes from a very different social world all the way across Canada. Jocelyn has just expressed a certain feminist opinion, and then we read the following:

> These were the ideas of most well-educated, thoughtful, even unconventional or politically radical young women of the time. One of the reasons Rose did not share them was that she had not been well educated. Jocelyn said to her, much later in their friendship, that one of the reasons she found it so interesting to talk to Rose, from the start, was that Rose had ideas but was uneducated. Rose was surprised at this, and mentioned the college she had attended in Western Ontario. Then she saw an embarrassed withdrawal or regret, a sudden lack of frankness in Jocelyn's face—very unusual with her—that that was exactly what Jocelyn had meant.

See Munro, *The Beggar Maid* (1978; New York: Penguin, 1980), 107.

2. Gerald Graff, *Professing Literature: An Institutional History* (Chicago: University of Chicago, 1987), 2.

3. Vladamir Nabokov, *Pnin* (1957; New York: Vintage, 1989), 9.

4. One of the few is Paul Fussell, in a book rather inevitably titled *Class*. But the point about his reading is that, first, it's easier to read others reading; so he amusingly quotes from an edition of *The New York Times Selective Guide to American Colleges* in order to compare the ratings to those of the *Guide Michelin*. (For example, four stars for a college roughly equals two for cuisine, far more efficiently signifying "*Table excellente, merite un detour.*") See Fussell, *Class* (New York: Summit Books, 1983), 130. Secondly, he mentions "denominated" universities that were formerly state colleges and teacher's colleges, only to sneer at them, for in fact they are engaged in "ripping off the proles" (Fussell, 135). Another's critique of American higher education is cited: "The educational system has been effectively appropriated by the upper strata and transformed into an instrument which tends to reproduce the class structure and transmit inequality." However, the whole tone and direction of Fussell's presentation is to provide, finally, still another reproduction of the same structure

and therefore another transmission of its inequality. Compare Richard Ohmann, when he quotes Gramsci in order to write virtually the same statement that Fussell approvingly cites. See Ohmann, *The Politics of Letters* (Middletown: Wesleyan University Press, 1987), 8. The quandary of employing the evaluative instruments of first-rate institutions, which are the only ones there are, without necessarily approving of them is rather better avoided in fictional texts. Early in *Libra* the semi-retired CIA agent, Win Everett, is visited at the college to which he has been exiled by two of his former colleagues. "My God, they buried you," the men utter. To which Everett replies, with, one presumes, some irony: "Texas Woman's University. Savor the name" (DeLillo, *Libra* [New York: Viking, 1988], 19).

5. Stanley Fish, "Reply," *PMLA* 104, no. 2 (March 1989): 220.

6. Gilbert and Gubar, "The Man on the Dump Versus the United States of America; or, What Does Frank Lentricchia Want?" *Critical Inquiry* 14, no. 2 (Winter 1988): 404.

7. Pierre Bourdieu, *Distinction* (Cambridge: Harvard University Press, 1987), 463. Many pages of Stanley Watkins's *Work Time: English Departments and the Circulation of Cultural Values* (Stanford: Stanford University Press, 1989) could of course be profitably read because of their implication in precisely such a discourse, although, as I have already suggested, Watkins's very notion of academic work suffers because it has no institutional specificity or interinstitutional depth.

8. Richard Ohmann's *English in America* (New York: Oxford University Press, 1976) has a nice example, amid a discussion of "the familiar hierarchy of institutions." Ohmann quotes the following from *ADE Bulletin*: "If an applicant presents a *summa* degree from Harvard, shall we say, it is unlikely that anybody will ask for supporting evidence. If, on the other hand, he presents straight A's from Slippery Rock . . ." (Ohmann, 231). Ohmann mentions that fictitious examples of "the boondocks" are more commonly given, but doesn't attempt to unpack this practice. (Because "a world of haves and have-nots" is just taken for granted?) Most unfictitious Slippery Rock is Clarion's rival, less than an hour away.